THE
INN AT LITTLE
WASHINGTON

Guests can tell they have arrived at a place where extraordinary food is served in warm, comfortable surroundings.

Also in the Great Restaurants of the World series:

Café des Artistes
Charlie Trotter's
Commander's Palace
The Sardine Factory

THE INN AT LITTLE WASHINGTON

An Insider's Look at the Famed Restaurant and Its Cuisine

Jay Levin

Photographs by Tim Turner

Lebhar-Friedman Books

New York • Chicago • Los Angeles • London • Paris • Tokyo

Lebhar-Friedman Books
425 Park Avenue
New York, NY 10022

Published by Lebhar-Friedman Books
Lebhar-Friedman Books is a company of Lebhar-Friedman, Inc.

Printed in the United States of America

Library of Congress Cataloging-in-Publication Data

Levin, Jay
    The Inn at Little Washington : an insider's look at the famed
restaurant and its cuisine / Jay Levin.
        p. cm. — (Great restaurants of the world)
    ISBN 0-86730-804-4 (alk. paper)
    1. Cookery, American. 2. Inn at Little Washington. I. Title.
II. Series.

    TX715.L6597 2000
    641.5973—dc21
                                        99-059967

Book design: Nancy Koch, NK Design

An SCI production

Jacket design: Kevin Hanek
Photographs © 2000 by Tim Turner

Visit our Web site at lfbooks.com

About the author

Jay Levin has been a magazine and newspaper writer and editor for more than 20 years, specializing in business and travel. He contributes to *Crain's New York Business, New Jersey Monthly Magazine,* Woman's Day Special Interest Publications, Selling Communications, and many business travel publications. He has worked for *Meetings & Conventions,* the *San Diego Tribune, The Record* of Hackensack, New Jersey, and other newspapers. A graduate of the University of Michigan, he lives in Bogota, New Jersey, with his wife and two children.

About the photographer

Tim Turner is a Chicago photographer who has been acclaimed for his cookbook photography and for his work in food advertising. Among the cookbooks he has contributed to are *The Inn at Little Washington Cookbook, Jacques Pepin: Encore with Claudine,* and a series by the Chicago chef Charlie Trotter. In 1998, Turner received the James Beard Award for Photography for *Charlie Trotter's Desserts.*

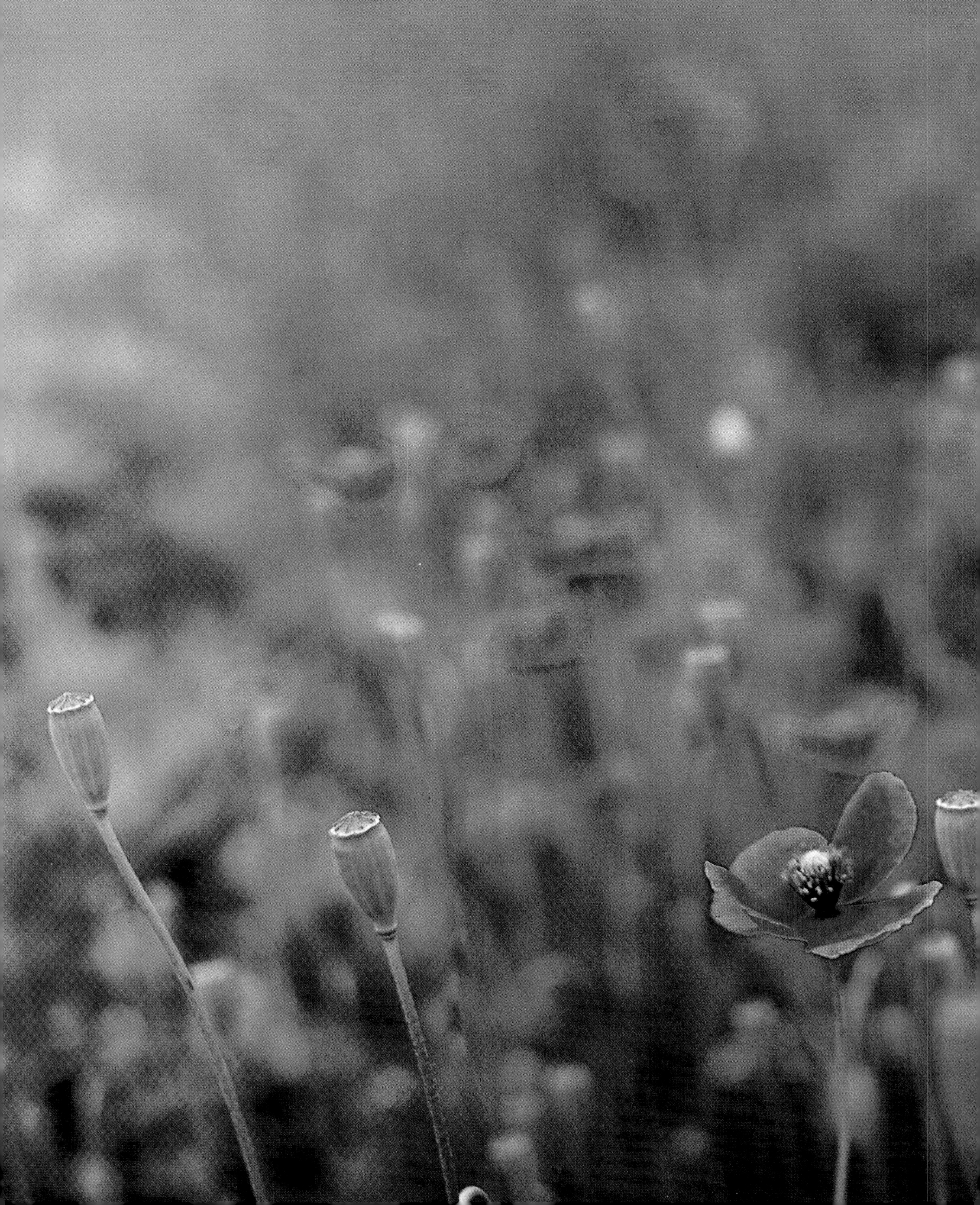

CONTENTS

FOREWORD

Few experiences in life enhance the joy of living more than a fine dining experience. The ambience, style, service, food, and presentation of a great restaurant are all elements that add immensely to enjoying a culinary adventure. Many restaurants provide customers with a consistent dining experience, and a number of these are truly outstanding. Only a few, however, exceed the expectations of even their most discerning patrons. They deserve to be called great, and we are proud to recognize them

as Great Restaurants of the World. The first five restaurants in this series of books are:

The Inn at Little Washington
Café des Artistes
Charlie Trotter's
Commander's Palace
The Sardine Factory

These beautiful books have been a labor of love and dedication for all the parties involved. We have called upon the editors of *Nation's Restaurant News,* the leading business publication serving the restaurant industry, to assist us in developing the criteria for the Great Restaurants of the World series and in choosing the candidates. We think you will agree that the selections are of great interest and merit.

All of the Great Restaurants of the World represent a unique creative spirit of providing the public with a meaningful dining experience. However, they also share many of the same traits. Most significantly, each was founded by one or more persons with the kind of entrepreneurial energy dedicated to achieving excellence. Without exception, these founders instilled in their organizations a single compelling mission: to provide their guests with the ultimate dining experience. Food and food presentation are always the first priority. After that come service, ambience, and value.

All of these restaurants have been successful by paying attention to innumerable small details every day, every week, and every month throughout the year. Each has proved many times over its reputation as a truly great restaurant through the loyalty of its repeat customers and the steady stream of awards and recognition it has received over the years, both from its guests and from its peers.

This book and the others in the series are your invitation to experience the Great Restaurants of the World, their history and their heritage. Savor every page and enjoy the adventure.

James C. Doherty
Executive Vice President
Lebhar-Friedman, Inc.

Awards

Following are some of the awards that have been presented to The Inn at Little Washington:

Mobil Five Star
For the Inn—1989-2000
For the restaurant—1991-2000
The Inn was the first property to receive five stars in both categories.

AAA Five Diamond
For the restaurant—1989-2000
For the Inn—1990-2000

Relais & Châteaux—member since 1987; presented with the Relais Gourmand distinction in 1989.

James Beard Awards
Best Chef in the Mid-Atlantic Region 1993
Restaurant of the Year 1993
Best Service Award 1997
Best Wine List Award 1998

Nation's Restaurant News
Fine Dining Hall of Fame 1991

Cigar Aficionado
Grand Cru Award 1999

Wine Spectator
Grand Award 1996-1999

Gourmet
Top Tables Award 1997-1999
Rooms at the Top 1999

Robb Report
Top Five Properties 1999

Travel & Leisure
Top 100 Properties 1999

Andrew Harper
Top Five U.S. Resort Hideaways 1998-1999
Top 15 U.S. Resort Hotels 1998-1999

The main reason O'Connell and Lynch have made the Inn a resounding success: It's their life.

The Inn at Little Washington

CHAPTER ONE

WHERE GUESTS CAN HAVE IT ALL WHEN THEY GET AWAY FROM IT ALL

Route 211 slices a swath through Virginia's magnificent Shenandoah Valley, all rolling hills and grassy pastures. Sixty-five miles west of, but light-years away from, the nation's capital, a blue sign at the turnoff for tiny Washington, Virginia, announces a huge hospitality understatement: FOOD LODGING.

A short way off the highway, at the corner of Main and Middle streets, cater-corner from the redbrick post office and within view of the Blue Ridge Mountains, stands a columned, pale-green building adorned with flags, the only purveyor of both food and lodging in this rustic community. One has to strain to make out the words on the plaque at the entrance, which reads simply, "The Inn at Little Washington."

Food and lodging, indeed, are the stock in trade at The Inn at Little Washington, but the terms no more do justice to the place than the word *transportation* adequately describes a Rolls-Royce. The Inn sees little need to call undue attention to itself, however. It has spent not a dime on advertising since it opened in 1978.

This country inn's intimate, 80-seat restaurant serves up a dining experience so sublime, so full of generous surprises, so steeped in perfection that it sets even well-traveled gourmets agog. British composer Andrew Lloyd Webber has called

Most patrons must drive an hour or more to get there, but the Inn's telephone operators routinely field hundreds of dinner reservation requests for any evening.

The Inn at Little Washington his favorite restaurant in the United States. Dining-survey publisher Tim Zagat lauds it as that rare restaurant that does everything right — "the food, the decor, the service, all done with real style and absolute quality." It is telling, perhaps, that Zagat, whose eponymous maroon-colored guides are standard equipment for gastronomes, says the Inn "is the one place in the world I've had trouble getting a table."

Here's why: Everyone else has the same idea. The Inn's telephone operators routinely field hundreds of dinner reservation requests for a particular evening. This for a place nearer to the rugged splendor of Shenandoah National Park than to the bustling confines of the Washington Beltway, its primary market. So impeccable is the Inn's reputation that customers think nothing of traveling an hour or more to have dinner there. Those with ample budgets usually stay overnight in one of the Inn's 14 sumptuous guest rooms rather than brave the dark drive home on a full stomach.

The Inn's food is well worth the drive. In the plush, softly lit dining room, seven courses of imaginative fare, influenced by classical French cuisine but redolent of the flavors of Virginia cookery, are borne by servers who glide silently between kitchen and customer. Many of chef Patrick O'Connell's dishes have become classics, among them chilled grilled black mission

In the Shenandoah Valley, life slows to a hospitable pace.

At the start, "every indicator pointed to failure: no money, no location, no customers," says dining critic Alan Richman. "The interesting question isn't How did they succeed? but Why didn't they fail?"

figs with country ham and lime cream, a signature first course, and crispy seared foie gras on polenta with country ham and blackberries, an example of how O'Connell adeptly melds elegant and mundane ingredients. One of his most famous desserts is My Grandmother's Rhubarb Pizza, a cheeky tribute to the person who inspired him at an early age. His Seven Deadly Sins provides a decadent dessert choice for the indecisive.

But delectable food is just part of the show. And what a show it is, for dinner at The Inn at Little Washington is like a night at the theater. Tuxedoed waiters, so eager to please that the word *no* has been strick-

Fresh produce from the Virginia countryside and flowers from its own garden are hallmarks of the Inn.

A Setting Both Idyllic and Historic

Before there was a Washington, D.C., there was a Washington, Virginia, surveyed and laid out in 1749 by a resilient teenager in the employ of Lord Fairfax. Or so they say. That teenager was George Washington, and the Shenandoah Valley hamlet was the first of many to bear his name. Historical markers proclaim, "The First Washington of All."

Some natives are skeptical, however. "Never let the truth get in the way of a damn fine story," says burly, bearded John W. McCarthy, administrator of Rappahannock County, of which Washington is the governmental seat. "I find the evidence less than convincing."

Regardless of who plotted it, Washington's two-by-five-block grid has stood the test of time. The original streets are still intact and bear such names as Jett, Wheeler, Calvert, and Gay—those of the families that owned the land on which the town was founded.

Lining the streets are fine old homes built of clapboard and log, some housing art galleries and gift shops patronized by those who drive out to relax and dine at The Inn at Little Washington. The Rappahannock National Bank occupies a stately building of yellow-painted brick on Gay Street, and across the street, the Rappahannock County offices are housed on a redbrick campus. The bell in the courthouse steeple rings six times a year, when the grand jury convenes. Over a bit is the county jail. The inmates are counted as part of the town's total population of 180.

This Washington is so peaceful that traffic control is not required. In fact, there is nary a stoplight in all of Rappahannock County, home to just 7,000 Virginians and one world-class restaurant.

en from their vocabulary, go about their business with precision. Plates accented in gold are set before each group of guests at exactly the same moment. Even the crumbing of the table, accomplished with a few strokes of a folded napkin, has a certain drama to it.

As at any hit show, scanning the clientele usually reveals a celebrity or two. Paul Newman, Barbra Streisand, and Alan Greenspan are among the glitterati who consider an evening at the Inn one of life's pleasures. Nearly every night, a handful of special occasions, such as wedding anniversaries, birthdays, and marriage proposals, are celebrated here. For suitors hoping to become engaged, the waiters are happy to serve as co-conspirators and are proficient at secreting diamond rings in a fresh oyster, a caramel cage, or amid rose petals scattered on a plate.

The story of The Inn at Little Washington is that of the two men who have poured their lives into the enterprise, O'Connell and his partner Reinhardt Lynch. After years of operating a catering service in northern Virginia's hunt country, the self-taught chef and the self-taught businessman opened their restaurant in the snowy winter of 1978. The building was a circa-1900 structure that had served the town variously as a social hall, a general store, and an automotive garage.

The youthful pair cleared the initial financial hurdles with relative ease. They started the Inn with $5,000 in savings, a loan approved by a bank officer familiar with O'Connell's cooking, and faith that cus-

The Inn's eclectic taste contributes to the cultural life of a town proud of its heritage.

It is a friendly, lighthearted place where the cooks honor the owners' pets by wearing Dalmatian-print pants.

tomers would eventually find their way to the restaurant and like what they tasted.

On the surface, it was not a recipe for success. "I think the interesting question isn't How did they succeed? but Why didn't they fail?" says Alan Richman, a nationally known dining critic. "Every indicator pointed to failure: no money, no location, no customers."

From the beginning, however, O'Connell and Lynch had something crucial: uncommonly good taste. Customers were warmly greeted at the door by Lynch, the maître d'. Inside the dining room, the basket-shade chandeliers cast a romantic glow, and the tables and chairs were of fine cherrywood. Fresh flowers were everywhere, even in the rest rooms. And O'Connell's intensely flavored food (aspic-glazed mousse of duck, and timbales of fresh crabmeat and spinach mousse were among the early entrées) was astonishing for so new and remote a restaurant. Within a few weeks, the dining critic from the *Washington Star* was rhapsodizing over his several visits, and this provided the impetus for the Inn's rise.

There have been numerous milestones on the Inn's road to becoming a legend. In the early 1980s, a sweeping redecoration by a British stage-set designer seemed appropriate, given O'Connell's earlier training in the theater. In 1985, the first eight guest rooms were opened, and two years later came affiliation with the prestigious Relais & Châteaux collection of luxury accommodations and restaurants. By 1991, Mobil Five-Star and AAA Five-Diamond ratings for both food and lodging had been bestowed on

Starting point for a cuisine flavored by French tradition but rooted in Virginia soil.

the Inn, along with an unprecedented near-perfect 29-29-29 rating in the *Zagat Restaurant Survey*. In 1996, O'Connell's *The Inn at Little Washington Cookbook—A Consuming Passion* was well received. In 1997, a gleaming new kitchen blending old-world touches and turn-of-the-21st-century wizardry provided the centerpiece for a $5-million expansion.

Under the exacting eyes of O'Connell and Lynch, The Inn at Little Washington has grown and prospered, collecting awards along the way, including the James Beard Foundation's citation as Restaurant of the Year in 1993. The road has not always been smooth. As its acclaim mounted, the Inn endured rocky relations with the little town it began to dominate. But throughout the Inn's development, the owners have stayed close to home and vigorously played their respective roles. Lynch remains the indefatigable host, overseeing his guests' comfort and directing the attentive staff. O'Connell excels as the artist who steadfastly believes that his place is in the kitchen, not on the hustings.

Although their establishment is known the world over, the owners manage to keep things in a healthy perspective. Yes, The Inn at Little Washington is expensive. Depending on the evening, the fixed-price seven-course dinner costs $98 to $128. But the place is also friendly and lighthearted, and the waiters never forget a name. Dessert sorbets are served in little paint jars, with spoons sticking out, on a clear artist's palette. The owners' Dalmatian, Rose, wears a pearl choker around her neck, and the cooks honor her and her mate, DeSoto, by wearing Dalmatian-print pants. Instead of do-not-disturb signs, overnight guests can ensure their privacy with tiny pillows embroidered with a curt—and highly original—directive.

After all, at its heart The Inn at Little Washington is just a tasteful country guesthouse tucked away in the Shenandoah Valley.

Besides restaurant awards, the Inn has been recognized for the comfort and good taste of its guest rooms.

O'Connell and Lynch started out by selling vegetables from their garden.

The Inn at Little Washington

CHAPTER TWO

THE ARTIST AND THE BUSINESSMAN

Reinhardt Lynch once offered an insightful explanation of how he and Patrick O'Connell combine their talents. "This is a team of the artist and the businessman," he said. "You can ask Patrick what somebody ate a year ago, and he'll be able to tell you in great detail. Ask him how much business we did a year ago, and he doesn't have a clue."

The artist and the businessman have scaled the heights of their profession, winning nearly every accolade worth having. Not bad for a couple of children of the sixties who once made ends meet peddling vegetables from their farm. There is no fancy culinary degree on O'Connell's résumé, no business degree on Lynch's. Their classroom has been the little Shenandoah Valley hideaway they struggled to open, their success the product of fastidious planning, long hours, and the determination to learn from others.

"I've always maintained that if you aim high and squint and look to the best role models, you've got a good shot at succeeding," says O'Connell. "It helps to realize that other humans have been able to achieve some remarkable feats."

But O'Connell and Lynch added something to the formula: unflinching, hands-on perfectionism.

The owners are front and center, sweating the details and demanding that others do likewise.

The new kitchen was designed to O'Connell's specifications.

Simply put, good is never good enough, lapses are not tolerated, and the owners themselves are front and center, sweating the smallest details and demanding that others do likewise.

"A lot of other celebrity chefs come in, yell at everyone, then go home and count their money," observes a former member of the dining room staff, "but these guys are right here every day, fluffing the curtains, fussing with the flowers, training the staff." In the process, O'Connell and Lynch have built an institution that faithfully reflects their good taste and sensibility, and theirs alone. "It's their world we're a part of," says Eric Brass, a longtime waiter, "and we're very proud to be a part of that world."

O'Connell and Lynch are an incongruous pair. Tall and lanky with honey-colored hair, O'Connell is a showman in chef's whites. His manner is engaging and dramatic, his words as exquisitely crafted as his food. Yes, he acknowledges, he has a gift. "Sometimes you don't feel like being the vehicle for the gift," he says. "You wish you could shut it off, but other times it is a great joy." As the creative force in the multimillion-dollar kitchen, O'Connell is the Inn's representative to the world, the one who signs the cookbooks and gives the interviews. Lynch, more reserved and plainspoken, is the ever-present host and behind-the-scenes numbers man. He is as comfortable making small talk with guests in the dining room he patrols nightly as he is making sense of the Inn's tax bill. The businessman's contribution is easy to overlook but no less integral to the Inn's growing legend.

Members of the postwar baby boom generation, both partners were born into large families, O'Connell in

High Art, Low Profile

Patrick O'Connell is a rarity these days: a celebrated chef who shuns celebrity. Unlike many top culinary professionals, O'Connell, winner of the James Beard Foundation's Best Chef Award/Mid-Atlantic and later a nominee for the foundation's Outstanding Chef Award, does not have a publicist and does not cut deals to endorse products. Although he grants interviews, his face is not all over the airwaves or on barbecue sauce labels. His most visible outside venture, *The Inn at Little Washington Cookbook,* spotlights the Inn, not the man. Referring to chefs who reinvent themselves as marketing conglomerates, one employee says, "That's just not Patrick."

The low profile is partly O'Connell's nature. "I'm not the star of the performance, unlike some other American chefs who think they are," he says. Then there are the day-to-day demands of being chef and co-owner. "There are always a thousand things to check," he says, "always something needing repair, always new products that have to be looked over, and the questions, questions, questions. I cannot really rest until the details are tended to. They all affect the guest experience."

People come to The Inn at Little Washington expecting O'Connell to be in the kitchen, and they are not disappointed. A glass of diluted iced tea always within reach, he oversees the cooking staff and signs off on plates at the chef's station. The showplace kitchen, with its bay windows, limestone fireplace, and mammoth, dark-green Vulcan range suite, is his realm.

That O'Connell believes his place is in the kitchen, not the TV studio, has won him admirers. John Mariani, the food writer, says, "Patrick is always in his kitchen. He once explained it to me this way: 'The guys I have working for me have been here for years, yet every night I walk through my kitchen and see 30 things I want to correct.'"

Daniel Maye, executive vice president of the International Association of Culinary Professionals, has his own theory about why O'Connell doesn't venture far from the Inn. Maye knows O'Connell must be toiling ceaselessly because he does not see him at industry events attended by other notable chefs. "He has a commitment to perfection and excellence," Maye says, "but I think he also has a hard time delegating and probably needs to be there because he feels he can do the job better than anyone else."

O'Connell's realm.

1945 and Lynch in 1947. Each had a taste of restaurant work in his teens, although their ambitions would not turn serious until their collaboration a decade later.

Raised in the Maryland suburbs of Washington, D.C., O'Connell was 15 when he landed an after-school job in a take-out joint. The bill of fare consisted of steak sandwiches, homemade potato salad and coleslaw, batter-dipped onion rings, and the like. O'Connell worked the grill, served the food, and loved every minute. "The people who worked there were fascinating to me—so abnormal, so unusual," he recalls. "They had bizarre lives, much like carnival or circus people."

Inventive cooking was not a priority in the O'Connell home. "My mom was a modern fifties housewife who always cooked in high heels," O'Connell says. Thus, the man who does wondrous things with snowy fillets of Chilean sea bass and trout pulled from local streams remembers frozen fish sticks as a Friday-night staple. Was his mother a good cook? "I always say she was a wonderful hostess," he says mischievously.

For inspiration, the future chef turned to his grandmother in Wisconsin, who was adept at "making something out of nothing," whether it was a simple piece of meat or the rhubarb stalks she grew in her yard. Young Patrick cooked with her during summer vacations, and years later he honored her memory by placing My Grandmother's Rhubarb Pizza on the Inn's dessert menu.

His grandmother saw O'Connell as a doctor or an architect, but Patrick, moved by the work of Swedish film director Ingmar Bergman, had other plans: "I wanted to write, I wanted to act, I wanted to do films." Scholarship in hand, he went off to study speech and acting at Washington's Catholic University. But the per-

Virginia's fashionable hunt country
is near Shenandoah National Park.

A favorite first course:
carpaccio of baby lamb on arugula.

formances that enraptured him unfolded not on the stage but in the dining rooms of the restaurants where he waited tables to help finance his education. "I found that it is like being in the middle of two plays at once," he says. "You have the drama behind the scenes in the kitchen and the drama going on in the dining room, and they are hilarious when juxtaposed against each other."

Lynch's introduction to restaurant work was as a busboy in the catering department at Purdue University in his hometown of Lafayette, Indiana. Unlike O'Connell's first job, Lynch's had a touch of glamour: The clientele and the food were upscale, and Lynch got to dress up. "It was a whole universe I was not accustomed to, and I loved it," he says.

At Indiana University, Lynch majored in French and spent his junior year studying in Brussels. Graduating at the height of the Vietnam War and seeing many friends go to Canada to escape the draft, he successfully applied for conscientious- objector status and served as an orderly in a Washington, D.C., hospital.

It was in Washington that Lynch and O'Connell met through friends. His schooling over, O'Connell had returned from extended travels in Europe, where he had developed an appreciation of the power of the dining experience and was overwhelmed by the French reverence for good food. Chefs in France, he wrote in *The Inn at Little Washington Cookbook,* "were taken as seriously as performing artists or athletes were in the States. The admiration of great restaurants approached religious fervor."

O'Connell was living on a farm in Virginia's tony hunt country, near Shenandoah National Park. He devoured cookbooks checked out from the library in the nearest town and grew organic vegetables. His woodstove was fired daily, and friends became the beneficiaries of his burgeoning passion. In time, Lynch, his wartime obligation fulfilled and with no particular career in mind, joined O'Connell on the farm. There wasn't a lot of work in the area, but they scraped by, doing odd jobs and selling the bounty from their garden.

Happenstance brought the pair their professional break. James J. Kilpatrick, the newspaper columnist and conservative voice on the Point-Counterpoint segment on *60 Minutes,* gave a lift to a hitchhiker and mentioned that he needed help with yard work on his Rappahannock County estate. The hitchhiker knew just the guys. O'Connell and Lynch were only too happy to cut Kilpatrick's grass and weed his garden, and they each earned $18 a week for their trouble.

"Neither of them knew anything about machinery, but they were willing and friendly," Kilpatrick says. So willing, in fact, that when the columnist's wife lamented that she could use a hand washing dishes after a dinner party, the grass-cutters jumped at the chance.

"We put on white shirts and bow ties—the shirts were from Goodwill—washed the dishes, and cleaned up the house afterward," Lynch says. The Kilpatricks entertained regularly, and the young men swiftly worked their way up from the kitchen sink.

For one party, O'Connell offered to make the Kilpatricks a watercress soup. "Just a beautiful, beautiful soup," the columnist says, savoring the memory. "A few weeks later, we were giving another party, and Patrick volunteered to do the dessert." While

O'Connell saw to the tarts, Lynch parked the guests' cars. "By that time," Kilpatrick says, "we were Patrick and Reinhardt fans."

Kilpatrick and his wife could not keep a good thing to themselves. "It's very gossipy in the hunt country," he says, "and when word spread that these hard-working guys, one of them a marvelous cook, could be had to cater parties and luncheons, it was onward and upward for them."

Building on word of mouth, the pair opened O'Connell-Lynch Caterers, which they ran from the farmhouse. O'Connell cooked on the old woodstove and used an electric frying pan that he'd picked up at a yard sale. Supplies came mainly from a Safeway supermarket 40 miles away. Despite the humble trappings, extravagance was their hallmark from the beginning, and cost was no object. Whether catering a small dinner gathering or a wedding ball for hundreds, they never stinted, even renting caged birds as table decor and paying for them out of their own pockets. "We wanted ours to look like parties people had never seen before," Lynch says, and the young men achieved their goal. Soon, they became a legend among the hunt country elite.

Going all out had its price, however. The catering business was not bringing in enough money, and stomping through the Virginia countryside was exhausting. Wouldn't it be better, they thought, if the customers came to them? That meant opening a restaurant. But not just *any* restaurant.

O'Connell's theory is that people work better in a beautiful kitchen.

The Inn at Little Washington

CHAPTER THREE

FROM COUNTRY STORE TO "NOUVELLE RAPPAHANNOCK"

A place like The Inn at Little Washington doesn't happen overnight. Patrick O'Connell and Reinhardt Lynch bided their time after setting a goal of opening a grand country restaurant. They systematically laid the groundwork through the late 1970s, visiting numerous establishments for inspiration and even picking up a 900-piece set of china at auction four years in advance.

Determining that they could use practical experience, the partners phased out their catering business (Senator John Warner and his wife, Elizabeth Taylor, were their final clients) and went to work for others. Their key apprenticeship was at a venerable French restaurant, L'Auberge Chez François, in Great Falls, Virginia. O'Connell was a chef and Lynch worked in the dining room under the exacting eye of owner Francois Haeringer, who had started in downtown Washington, D.C., a generation earlier.

L'Auberge Chez François was an exceptional training ground and Haeringer an exceptional teacher. "I learned from him that a restaurant had to be run in a businesslike manner," Lynch recalls. "Tardiness was not tolerated; there were contingency plans if someone from the dining room staff was sick; every bottle of wine was kept track of." Haeringer remembers the pair as conscientious and ambitious employees. "They wanted to learn the trade," he says, "and they succeeded."

After more than a year of searching for a location,

Guests are often surprised by the finery behind the Inn's modest facade. At right, the entrance in 1983.

Photograph by Louise van Dort

37

O'Connell and Lynch settled on Washington, Virginia, a bucolic but listless town whose borders had not expanded beyond the same five-by-two-block grid surveyed by George Washington in 1749. The Rappahannock County seat, Washington was an ideal spot—far enough from the other Washington to qualify as "country" but not so distant as to make a resident of Bethesda or Arlington think twice about driving out for dinner.

A few years earlier, Route 211 had bypassed the town, diverting traffic from the sturdy old homes and redbrick government offices at its core. The gabled turn-of-the-century building that O'Connell and Lynch had in mind was at the corner of Main and Middle streets. It had variously been Thornton's Garage, a community recreation hall, and most recently, a craft shop called The Country Store. Over the years, townsfolk had gathered there to celebrate the end of World War I, to watch silent movies, and to play basketball. Now, this building so important to the social life of the town would become a mecca of fine dining.

A lease-purchase agreement was struck in which the owners of the building would get a percentage of the restaurant's gross receipts as rent. But before the papers were signed, Lynch was overcome with second thoughts. "My gut feelings about business had started to click," he says. "If we weren't successful, it would be a moot point, but if we were successful, we would regret the day we took them in as partners."

Eventually, a new deal was reached in which O'Connell and Lynch would pay $200 a month rent for the first two years and then purchase the building for a price set at the time of the agreement. To this day, O'Connell and Lynch, the only owners The Inn at Little Washington has ever known, have steadfastly avoided the risk of compromising their independence.

Another hurdle followed, however. The men had little more than $5,000 in savings between them. They would need a $50,000 bank loan for renovation and start-up costs. The one bank in town had a $25,000 lending limit, so the would-be restaurateurs looked to the bank in Warrenton, 20 miles away. As luck would have it, the bank president had attended parties arranged by O'Connell-Lynch Caterers. The check was cut the next day.

The Inn at Little Washington opened on the evening of February 1, 1978, amid one of the snowiest spells in memory. The 40-seat dining room, with its

Photograph by Louise van Dort

Who could have imagined that one day they'd be steaming lobster above the grease pit?

Snow, rarely heavy in the valley, complicated opening night in February 1978.

cherrywood tables and chairs, crewel-patterned carpeting, and basket-like hanging lampshades, bore no resemblance to the building's previous incarnations. The kitchen stood over where the mechanic's pit had been. The small staff was composed of local residents, including one waiter in combat boots spray-painted black. Most of the entrées were priced between $6 and $8, the roast chicken with tarragon a steal at $4.95. Fortunately, O'Connell and Lynch already had a customer base—their former catering clients who lived in the area. Then, two hours before the first guests were to arrive, O'Connell, wracked by abdominal pains, sought refuge under Table 11. Appendicitis, he thought. Opening-night nerves, it turned out.

The following week, the restaurant's opening was heralded on the front page of the weekly *Rappahannock News*. A long-haired, mustached O'Connell, wearing chef's whites, and a conservatively coifed Lynch in a three-piece suit, were pictured in the kitchen and in the dining room. For more than 1,000 words, reporter Daphne McCullough chronicled the proprietors' conversion of the former Country Store and their plans for the business. "We hope it will be somewhere to get away from the harsh realities of life," O'Connell was quoted as saying. In a bit of prophetic editorializing, McCullough concluded, "The Inn should be a resounding success."

Another journalist, dining columnist John Rosson of the *Washington Star,* was a repeat customer during the first few weeks. Rosson, who had a weekend home nearby, had noticed the renovation work at the corner of Main and Middle and thought he would try the Inn. His hopes were not high. After all, who would be dumb enough to open a restaurant way out here in ragged little Washington, Virginia? Rosson figured it would be "a hot dog place or something."

It wasn't. His glowing review opened the floodgates almost overnight. Phyllis Richman of the rival *Washington Post* followed with her own rave. The Inn was plunked squarely on the Washington, D.C., culinary map—perhaps earlier than anyone had expected, save O'Connell and Lynch. As word spread, the dining room filled up and the innkeepers raised their prices "in self-defense," O'Connell likes to say.

From the beginning, Washington, D.C.-area residents were willing to drive nearly to Shenandoah National Park for a memorable meal, but major restaurant purveyors were not. For several years, the Inn was virtually the only show in Rappahannock County, and the proprietors could not per-

Room for More Rooms At the Inn

*W*ashington, Virginia, was tattered around its pastoral edges when cabinetmaker Peter Kramer settled there in 1970, not long after the Route 211 bypass siphoned away traffic and, with it, any hopes of commercial vitality.

"The town was asleep," says Kramer, whose studio is around the corner from The Inn at Little Washington. "There were 20 buildings abandoned, maybe more. It was a storybook waiting for Prince Charming to show up."

Or, in this case, two Prince Charmings. In the 1980s, O'Connell and Lynch started buying and sprucing up building after building in the vicinity of the Inn. By the end of the next decade, they would own 17. Some house the Inn's back-office operations. The White House, which is yellow, has administrative offices. The telephone reservationists have their own building, the gardener and the florist another. One building provides temporary living quarters for new staff. Across the street from the Inn's flower beds is the owners' home, Rose Cottage, named for one of their Dalmatians and used occasionally for VIP accommodations.

These real estate acquisitions have enabled O'Connell and Lynch to influence the aesthetics of the town and to create, within the Inn, an environment dedicated to the care and feeding of guests. "The scope of our business would not have been possible without our buying these properties," says Lynch.

The buildings are also key to any future guest-room expansion. "Our rooms are sold out sometimes six, seven months in advance, which is an indication that there aren't enough of them," Lynch says. The owners won't be making the former Country Store any bigger, however. They've done that twice, and they like it the way it is. But across the street or around the corner and down the block—now that's a different matter.

Guest rooms are furnished to reflect the owners' notion of an English country house.

In quest of a $1-million expansion loan, the innkeepers had the good fortune to encounter a bank president with a taste for good cooking: The Inn was his favorite restaurant.

suade their suppliers to deliver to little Washington. So it fell to Lynch to set out before 3 a.m. several times a week and load up with supplies in big Washington. Returning in the early afternoon, he would nap briefly before getting ready for the evening's dinner customers. All in a day's labor for the hardworking restaurateurs, who were fast making a name for themselves.

One of O'Connell and Lynch's early luxuries was closing for several weeks in winter to visit the country inns of France. These pilgrimages influenced the Inn's menu and decor as well as the partners' philosophy of hospitality. "It was a heartwarming experience, and we thought, oh goodness, maybe we can do something close to what these people are doing—how they're taking care of their customers," Lynch says.

For O'Connell, the sojourns abroad were a rich source of inspiration. "We'd spend two or three days at each place, absorbing what we could, and come back refreshed and ready to undergo another year of hard labor," he says. "Each year, the gap narrowed between what they were doing and what we were doing, until finally it did not seem necessary to make those trips to France anymore."

The 1980s dawned with a sweeping redecoration done by Joyce Conwy Evans, a stage set designer from London and a friend of the Inn's local architect. With walls stippled in layers of soft peach, windows covered in lace café curtains, and generous use of the finest fabrics, Evans' design reflected the owners' vision of an inviting English country house. Especially dramatic was the coffered ceiling of the two-story entrance hall. With hundreds of cutouts from a wallpaper called Gothic Lily (it had been designed for the House of Lords), the effect was that of stained glass.

Evans' work was all the more remarkable in that she did not set foot in the Inn until years later. Architectural blueprints were sent to her in England, and she sent watercolor renderings back to Virginia. The furniture, wall coverings, and fabrics were purchased in England and numbered to be installed on site, like a jigsaw puzzle.

A major investment in the late 1990s was the state-of-the-art kitchen.

As the Inn's reputation and press clippings mounted (the *New York Times* reported on O'Connell's "Nouvelle Rappahannock" cuisine in 1983), more people outside the Washington Beltway clamored for tables, and inside the Beltway, more clamored for accommodations so they would not have to drive home late at night. A guest-room expansion was inevitable, but it would be expensive.

The Inn had outgrown its Warrenton bank, so O'Connell and Lynch, armed with architectural plans and deposits on rooms that did not exist, began calling on Washington, D.C., banks in quest of a $1-million loan. After a dispiriting series of cold shoulders, the innkeepers had the good fortune to encounter another bank president with a taste for good cooking: The Inn happened to be his favorite restaurant.

The first eight guest rooms opened in 1985. In the late 1990s, some $5 million was invested in an eye-popping new kitchen, two more guest suites, new public spaces called the Monkey Lounge and the Dining Room, and a new seating area called the Loggia.

Every year has brought new acclaim: membership in Relais & Châteaux, the prestigious worldwide organization of luxury restaurants and hotels, in 1987; an AAA Five-Diamond rating for dining in 1989 and for accommodations in 1990; a Mobil Five-Star rating for accommodations in 1989 and for dining in 1991; an astounding 29-29-29 rating in the 1991 *Zagat Survey;* a passel of James Beard Foundation awards throughout the 1990s, including Restaurant of the Year.

How The Inn at Little Washington will continue to evolve is by no means etched in stone. Additional guest quarters? Quite likely. An experimental low-fat menu? They're working on it. "It's important not to measure yourself by anyone's standards but your own," the chef asserts, "so the Inn's evolution has to mirror your own evolution." Of a certainty, though, Patrick O'Connell and Reinhardt Lynch will continue to strive mightily to fulfill the fantasies and exceed the expectations of the people who matter most: their guests.

A HARDHEADED BUSINESS DECISION

In 1990, The Inn at Little Washington boldly went where few restaurants have dared to go. It instituted a fixed-price menu, with higher prices on weekends ($58 before wine, tax, and tip) than on weeknights ($48). By the late 1990s, the price for dinner had risen to $98 Monday through Thursday, $108 on Friday and Sunday, and $128 on Saturday. Reinhardt Lynch says introducing a fixed price was a hard but necessary business decision because many customers were in the habit of splitting first courses or forgoing dessert. That cost the Inn revenue, especially on the most popular night, Saturday. "Do we add tables to make up the lost revenue?" Lynch asks rhetorically. "We didn't want to. The only choice was to go to a fixed-price menu, which had the effect of spreading out the business."

How did customers react? "They immediately started to relax," says Lynch. "There was no more 'Should I order the most expensive thing on the menu or the least expensive?' or 'Should I order the appetizer?' With one price for dinner, all those concerns evaporated."

Nowhere else on the planet can you find a celery root bisque like this.

Rolling countryside provides a tranquil backdrop to the Inn's bustle.

The Inn at Little Washington

CHAPTER FOUR

A PHILOSOPHY OF LUXURIOUS NEW-WORLD HOSPITALITY

Patrick O'Connell and Reinhardt Lynch have an unwritten compact with their customers. The Inn at Little Washington will stage an evening of sybaritic pleasures for them, but the guests, in O'Connell's words, "have their little mountain to climb, too."

Or, more accurately, their little highway to drive. "It's important to create a challenge for the guests," says O'Connell. "If they can just hop in a cab from any street corner and be to you in five minutes, what fun would that be? They have to put aside the whole evening, first of all. They cannot be on their way to the theater or trying to catch a plane. As Barbra Streisand once said, 'People don't dance when I sing.' The guests have to turn themselves over to you."

Placing themselves in the Inn's custody, guests enter a world of rich fabrics and fragrant flowers, of 18th-century French wall sconces and gold-trimmed plates, 17th-century oak floorboards and amethyst-studded ceilings. O'Connell and Lynch and their staff take it from there, fashioning an experience in which every detail has been carefully considered and resolved. "It is definitely a performance, a film in which the guest is the star," O'Connell says. "We are allowing them to have a set and a cast and weave their own fantasies into a wonderful little drama."

O'Connell knows that people who spend several hundred dollars on dinner for two have high expectations. So does he. The former drama student believes his guests should leave the dining room feeling "changed," the way they would feel "after a connection with a great artistic performance."

He naturally compares having dinner at the Inn to attending the theater, and he sees the dining room as the set and the waitstaff as the cast. The chef is a cast member, too, albeit one with production responsibilities. He is not the star, O'Connell insists. At this performance, top billing goes to the audience.

"It is important to understand the ultimate potential of the dining experience," he says. "It can be a life-changing, transcendental experience that takes you completely away from your own reality. It can raise your level of self-esteem, it can be a sort of healing process, and it can make you feel that life is worth living. That is what we aim for."

Comments from grateful diners reveal that the Inn is consistently on target. "One head of a big corporation says he comes here to renew his faith in humanity," O'Connell says. "I thought that was very touching. It was wonderful praise that encourages us to keep doing what we are doing, and do it better."

The innkeepers regard the guest experience as sacrosanct. Every plate of food, every glass of wine, every object

Teamwork is critical to perfecting every element of hospitality.

"It is definitely a performance,

on the table, every element of decor, every note of background music, and every word, action, or gesture by the staff contributes to making the guest feel cared for, enthralled, swept away.

Nothing is done halfway. Everything has to be the best. If the time of year calls for My Grandmother's Rhubarb Pizza and the sous-chef determines that the best rhubarb is an ocean away in The Netherlands, so be it. No expense is spared.

Most restaurants would balk at the sums that The Inn at Little Washington spends on certain things. Flowers, for instance. Floral arrangements are on every dinner table, in every guest room, in every public space, even in the rest rooms. Flowers, of course, are meant to be noticed. Napkins aren't. Nevertheless, the Inn spent $60,000 on 28-by-28-inch custom-dyed "lapkins" woven to order from Egyptian cotton.

"That purchase took a year-and-a-half to get going, because we had to schedule the loom time in England," general manager Scott Little says. "We didn't need to do this, but it's something the guests will figure out the minute they sit down."

O'Connell and Lynch go to painstaking lengths to set their

lm in which the guest is the star."
—*Patrick O'Connell*

FIVE-STAR AND STILL FUN

For so critically acclaimed an institution, The Inn at Little Washington can be downright playful. Whimsical touches abound, such as the Dalmatian-spotted pants worn by the cooks, a tribute to the owners' pets, Rose and DeSoto. Then there is the mural of monkeys in the bar. Why monkeys? Patrick O'Connell happens to like them.

Instead of do-not-disturb signs, overnight guests are provided with little pillows embroidered with the words "Go Away." Lighthearted menu inserts inform guests of the springtime invasion of flying beetles, and cheekily worded menu items catch the diners' attention ("A Portobello mushroom pretending to be a filet mignon").

The light touch goes hand in hand with the owners' belief that five-star and fun aren't mutually exclusive. "We take the work seriously, but we don't take ourselves seriously," O'Connell says. "We want the guest to feel that the experience can be amusing. Humor is such an important element, one often lacking in the great European-style restaurants. You feel you can't giggle or have a good time."

There is a sort of "control effect" in many traditional luxe restaurants, O'Connell says, but that is not part of the Inn's philosophy. "I think there is a backlash against that," he says. "Twenty years ago, people expected to be abused at a fancy French restaurant, particularly one in America. The menu was only in French, there was a dress code, and the waiters were haughty. You had the feeling they were sizing you up and trying to figure out your net worth. Often, a burden was placed on the diner. The diner's only burden should be to enjoy the experience—and hopefully be able to pay the check."

The Inn has no dress code, although most patrons honor the elegant surroundings with appropriate attire. The menu is in straightforward English. Rather than sporting the imperious-sounding title of sommelier, the person in charge of the wine program is called the wine director.

Waiters, while not of the "Hi-my-name-is-so-and-so" ilk, are as genuine and pleasant as they are professional. It is their home, and everyone invites the guests to get comfortable, have what they want, and, hey, even loosen up.

Striking a lighthearted mood in the Monkey Lounge.

establishment apart from other restaurants and inns, and their formula has produced an extremely successful business. But a big part of their success, and a cornerstone of their operating philosophy, is making The Inn at Little Washington seem less a business than a grand hospitable home tucked away in the countryside. There are no road signs pointing the way to the Inn. Save for a small bronze plaque that a passing motorist would have difficulty reading, nothing announces what dwells behind the door of the building at Main and Middle

Custom-woven napkins (opposite) and abundant flowers help set the tone.

streets. The charge-card stickers so many restaurants display are nowhere to be seen. The newspaper and magazine reviews are out of public view; the only raves on display are the hand-written comments in the guest book.

There is no listing in the Rappahannock County business directory for the Inn, either. The proprietors have never advertised, relying instead on word of mouth from satisfied customers. In an era in which corner groceries and enterprising teenagers have Web sites, the Inn does not have a presence in cyberspace.

Significantly, O'Connell and Lynch won't even hint at such things as revenue, profit, and the size of the average check totted up in their dining room. They are not obliged to do so, of course, because the Inn is privately held. But what good host would dream of dwelling on the economics of impeccable hospitality?

"The problem is, that gives people the wrong impression," says Lynch, keeper of the numbers. "The feeling here is that people are coming to someone's home, and the commercialism has to be kept outside, which we try so desperately hard to do."

Every surface is embellished in the cause of creating a beautiful environment.

PRICING A GASTRONOMICAL WORK OF ART

"We in America don't yet have a full understanding or appreciation of the power of the dining experience," Patrick O'Connell observes, "and a lot of that is attributable to the fact that the media don't regard it as an art form."

For O'Connell, that is an injustice of the first order. He maintains that in the public mind, "it is perfectly all right for someone to buy a $25-million canvas and stick it on their

wall, if they have the money to do so. Everyone thinks that person is a connoisseur. But if someone spends $1,000 on dinner for four, people think it is politically incorrect. The experience is seen as intangible, but in my opinion that makes it much greater in value. You can't replicate it, just as you can't get back a performance by Marlene Dietrich."

Although the Inn's prices might seem beyond the reach of the average person, they are in line with other great restaurants in this country and abroad. And, according to

O'Connell, a high percentage of his customers are people of moderate means who happen to appreciate excellent food.

On a Saturday night, the prix fixe dinner is $128, or $256 for two people. A bottle of wine—say, a modest French vintage costing $50—brings the total to $306. Add the state's 4.5 percent sales tax and the town's 2.5 percent meals and lodging tax and you're up to $327. Reward the dining room staff with a 20 percent gratuity and the evening's tab rises to $388. And that is being conservative. By selecting a slightly more expensive wine, a couple could easily leave $500 in their wake.

"People consider the price a factor," O'Connell says, "but deciding where you will dine is really a matter of priority. When people say they can't afford to come here, I look at their tennis shoes, which cost $125 and were made in some factory. It baffles me that people won't allow themselves to have this kind of once-in-a-lifetime experience, to have an entire staff of people coddle them and look after them. I think it's the bargain of the century."

O'Connell regards the fixed price of dinner as the cost of admission to a place where every gastronomical whim is indulged. "Once you gain admittance, whatever you want is perfectly acceptable," he says. "So if a guest asks how big the lobster is, we say, 'How big would you like it?' And if they eat their complete main course and say, 'That was so good I could eat another,' we bring another, no questions asked."

The Inn at Little Washington

CHAPTER FIVE

CONTEMPORARY CUISINE WITH A GLOBAL REACH

Asked whether he considers himself a "young chef" now that he is into his third decade professionally, the boyish Patrick O'Connell chuckles and thinks for a moment.

"I don't think of myself in terms of a certain age," he says finally, "but, sure, I think I am still thought of as being unpredictable and an unknown commodity; hard to pin down, a bit of a rebel, and still a little playful."

Not surprisingly, that is how others view The Inn at Little Washington's cuisine. After all, what's one to make of a repertoire that incorporates such disparate elements as foie gras and Chilean sea bass, huckleberries and morels, black-eyed peas and bok choy, country ham and frog's legs—some of which wind up in the same dish?

Taking a stab at it, *Washington Post* restaurant reviewer Phyllis Richman, who has been dining at the Inn longer than just about anybody, calls it "American cuisine, with all the technique you'd expect from French cooking; while it can be complicated, it is not fussy." Yet, depending on who is doing the tasting, the Inn's cooking has also been dubbed French-American, contemporary American, new American, simple, eclectic, and *haute* regional.

O'Connell shies away from labels. "I don't care what people call it as long

Always inventive, O'Connell somehow manages to match his cuisine to the elegant surroundings.

as they enjoy it," he says. "You can skirt the issue by calling it personal or eclectic. It's like, how would you describe your personality in one word? It can't be done."

Officially, the Inn's menu states that the cooking, "while paying homage to the lawmakers of Classical French cuisine, reflects a belief in the 'cuisine of today'— healthy, eclectic, imaginative, unrestricted by ethnic boundaries, and always growing."

O'Connell expands on the theme. "We try to take whatever we can from the region and combine it in unique, amusing, innovative ways," he says. "We make it light and delicate and clean and reduce it to its essence. In the end, we give our guests something they cannot get anywhere else."

Hard-pressed to point to a single dish that summarizes his approach, O'Connell instead cites two. The first is foie gras with black-eyed peas vinaigrette, the foie gras chic and rich and the black-eyed peas a throwback to Southern slave cooking. The second is rabbit braised in apple cider, which the chef describes as "wonderfully hearty and suave and country and elegant, all at the same time." Both are mainstays of the menu.

Other longtime favorites at the Inn include foie gras on polenta with country ham and blackberries; medallions of veal Shenandoah; and timbales of crabmeat and spinach mousse, an ethereal dish introduced in the Inn's first year, 1978. For dessert, the intensely flavored white chocolate ice cream is so addictive that locals count on ordering it to go at the kitchen's back door.

The menu, which always has 10 to 15 selections, not only for the main course but for the first course and dessert as well, is anything but a rigid document. The availability of fresh provisions dictates changes daily. There are seasonal changes, too. Every fall, when local apple orchards are heavy with fruit, veal Shenandoah returns, slightly evolved from the year before. The dish started as a veal scallopini sauced with reduced apple cider but has been switched to medallions and endowed with a splash of Calvados cream.

Playful touches help relieve the pressure of running a
world-class kitchen.

O'Connell's dedication to the quality of ingredients is matched by his fidelity to Virginia products. Country ham, cured less than an hour away, turns up in numerous guises. Trout is caught in local streams, and rabbits are raised nearby. Rappahannock County morels appear during their all-too-brief season in the spring. Sassafras is scavenged for a palate-cleansing granita. Summer and fall bring a procession of growers to the kitchen door bearing peaches, tomatoes, apples, green beans, and pencil-thin asparagus. Sorrel, garlic, chives, tarragon, mint, and sage are snipped from the raised herb bed that John Testa, the Inn's gardener, tends just steps from the kitchen. In winter, of course, precious little comes from Virginia, save the ubiquitous country hams and other meats, but the indigenous spirit is ever present.

Similar care is lavished on the Inn's wine program, which boasts more than 1,000 selections and 15,000 bottles, mostly from France and California. Two dozen wines are available by the glass. Guests requesting the wine list are presented with a hefty document of more than 30 pages, but should they find the list bewildering, the waitstaff is schooled in the art of finding just the right wine to go with a meal.

"We must have the highest wine consumption per table in the industry," says Reinhardt Lynch. "Many nights there will be a full bottle, or multiple bottles, on every table." Diners with a hankering to uncork a 1900 Château d'Yquem, a Sauternes from a legendary year, are in luck—if they can afford the $10,000 price tag. But with selections in all price ranges, customers don't have to be concerned about breaking the budget when they order a good bottle of wine at The Inn at Little Washington.

Besides planning, the quest for perfect cookery entails collegial give-and-take between the chef and his staff. Every Friday,

Depending on who's doing the tasting, the Inn's cooking has been dubbed French-American, contemporary American, new American, simple, eclectic, or *haute* regional.

A Starring Role for Virginia Ham

Country ham is arguably Virginia's chief contribution to the culinary world, and The Inn at Little Washington has done its share to popularize this silken, down-home specialty. Rosy slivers of ham turn up between halves of little biscuits; curled around chilled, grilled figs; and mingled with risotto, shrimp, and oyster mushrooms. In one of Patrick O'Connell's most imaginative and popular first courses, the ham is teamed with a slab of seared foie gras, polenta, and fresh blackberries (*see* page 140); in a main course, the ham provides the filling for ravioli that accompanies pan-roasted tenderloin of veal and forest mushrooms.

The hams the Inn uses are delivered personally by the man who cures them, Tom Calhoun. "I live just a few miles down the road from the Inn," says the laconic Calhoun, who runs the family business, Calhoun's Ham House in Culpeper, Virginia.

Born in 1932, Calhoun learned the art of ham-curing from his uncle and started the business in 1970. He no longer raises his own hogs, instead acquiring hams from packers in Virginia and North Carolina. The hams, which run about 16 pounds, are rubbed with a mixture of salt and brown sugar and hung in the ham house for six months or more. The longer they cure, the saltier they get. "Patrick likes them not too salty," says Calhoun, who adjusts the process accordingly.

Throughout Virginia, Calhoun's hams are the basis for numerous church and firehouse fund-raising dinners, where groaning platters are passed around with bowls of mashed potatoes. This is the way most people know country ham; few are accustomed to encountering it cozied up to duck liver. "At one time, it did shock me that you can take country ham and serve it that way," says the man who delivers 200 hams a year to O'Connell's kitchen door.

Calhoun is struck by th
O'Connell combines Vir
unusual ingre

O'Connell's dedication to quality ingredients is matched by his fidelity to locally grown products.

O'Connell gathers his cooks, in their Dalmatian-print pants, around a table in the administrative White House to review the status of ingredients and brainstorm new menu items.

"We're not excited about the fava beans," one cook tells O'Connell, who orders them dropped from the dish in question. A hunk of cheese is sampled, the kitchen's attempt to make cheese from local sheep's milk. A lustrous slab of poached salmon on a tangle of greens, garnished with sorrel cream and halved cherry tomatoes, is passed around for tasting. O'Connell, who keeps a legal pad handy to jot notes and sketch dishes, deems the salmon not quite ready for guests. "It's isn't jelling," he says. "Try poaching it in celery juice and wine."

These meetings are central to the evolution of the Inn's cuisine but are not the only occasion for creative thought. O'Connell is constantly attuned to how the Inn's menu can be bolstered or a dish tweaked to make it even more remarkable. "You're always dealing with it on an unconscious plane," the chef says of menu planning, "when you sleep, when you are in the car, when you are waiting."

He and his cooks will tinker with a new idea for weeks or months before offering it to guests. One that has occupied them for some time is a "restorative menu" that, while still hewing to the Inn's standards, would be free of animal and milk fats, salt, sugar, and flour. Noting that the Inn's customers have wide-ranging tastes and health concerns, O'Connell wants to offer a selection of dishes for those "terrified" of salt and fat. "The idea is to have people feel mentally and physically rejuvenated after eating this food and in no way feel deprived," he says. "The courses must be stunning and intriguing and full of intense flavors, the ingredients distilled to their pure essence. Nothing you're putting into your body can be construed in any way as being negative."

The Perfect Set for an Extravaganza

hen the Inn's kitchen is at full throttle, the sound system pipes in the cadences of Gregorian chants. "That just seems right for the set," Patrick O'Connell says, "and it reduces the cursing."

The observation shows how seriously the Inn takes the theater where it creates unforgettable dishes of every description. For his first two decades as a restaurateur, O'Connell cooked in a yeomanly kitchen that seemed more cramped with each new accolade. "If you did more than 140 covers, you felt like you were dragged and run over because it was so physically challenging," the chef recalls.

Surely, the world-famous Inn at Little Washington needed a bigger kitchen, but the proprietors were loath to close down for weeks or months of construction. The solution was to build an entire kitchen wing with two second-floor guest suites that would provide some return on the seven-digit investment.

Of course, just any new kitchen would not do. It could not look like other restaurant kitchens, meaning it could not be bathed in institutional stainless steel. It would have to be comfortable for the cooks and pleasing to the Inn's guests. And it would have to be aesthetically faithful to a building that dates to 1900.

"Patrick wanted the nicest kitchen in America— one that looked like it had been there forever yet incorporated all the latest technology," says J. Russell LeBow Stilwell, a kitchen designer from Annapolis, Maryland, who oversaw the project.

More than two years in the planning and construction, it was a true collaboration. For inspiration, O'Connell and Stilwell leafed through books picturing old mansions and traveled to France to look at restaurant kitchens. British stage set designer Joyce Conwy Evans, the creative force behind the Inn's overall decor, was enlisted to work up sketches, which O'Connell and Stilwell followed to the finest line.

The result is a 2,100-square-foot showplace that is twice the size of the old kitchen. It has a 12-foot vaulted ceiling, a back-lit frieze above the moldings, hand-painted blue-and-white Portuguese wall tiles, and floor tiles set atop a thick layer of sand to be forgiving on the feet. Bay windows open onto the garden, and a cozy alcove has two pine tables flanking the limestone fireplace. O'Connell opens the tables to guests once in a while, making them the Shenandoah Valley's hottest ticket.

The biggest eye-opener is the marvel at the kitchen's center. The 15-by-7-foot Vulcan range suite, assembled in France according to O'Connell's specifications, is clad in forest-green baked enamel and fitted with polished brass handles and trim. Topping it off is a beveled copper hood decorated with a brass crown. "The shape of the hood was originally my idea, and Joyce added the crown," Stilwell says. "Its tapered shape is unusual for a modern kitchen; most range hoods are square."

Most range hoods, too, don't cost $30,000. This one did: $15,000 for the hood, another $15,000 for the crown. The entire kitchen wing, guest suites included, cost $3.5 million, or $1.5 million more than the owners had planned on.

Then again, the Inn didn't get where it is by sticking to a budget. "Investing this much money is a statement," O'Connell told an interviewer during construction. "It's unnecessary, but it shows a commitment and creates a feeling that [this business isn't] all about making money. If you provide a beautiful work environment, people are happier and perform much better."

More than two years in the making, the kitchen
is a showplace with a vaulted ceiling and a cozy
alcove for diners.

The Inn at Little Washington

CHAPTER SIX

A DINING EXPERIENCE THAT LEAVES NOTHING TO CHANCE

The pampering begins before customers reach the front door of The Inn at Little Washington. Those arriving for an overnight stay may think they are being abducted, so swift is the greeting. A strike force of formally attired waiters doubling as porters materializes to extend a welcome, spirit away luggage, and take custody of the automobile. The welcome is particularly dramatic in a rainstorm, when waiters, general manager Scott Little, and even co-owner Reinhardt Lynch descend on arriving patrons with huge umbrellas. Most customers have driven an hour or more for the meal of a lifetime, and the Inn is damned if the evening will begin with mussed hair or splattered clothing.

The greeting sets the tone for the hours to follow: highly attentive; friendly, but not overly personal; extravagant; theatrical!

For early-arriving dinner guests, the performance continues in either of the Inn's newest public spaces, the plush Living Room or the Monkey Lounge, named for the wall mural depicting simians engaged in music-making and other human

Lynch takes to heart the responsibility for making guests feel at home.

activities. The Living Room, which adjoins the kitchen and the dining areas, is the Inn's crossroads. Guests with a dinner reservation in the second wave of seating, between 8:30 and 9:30 p.m., can sip a drink by the fireplace and behold the silent parade of waiters bringing orders to the kitchen and carrying back the resulting creations. As choreographed as the waiters are in their movements as they pass through the Living Room, however, nothing compares to their performance on the "set."

Once guests have been escorted to their table and seated, they are presented with menus (that gentleman sliding out the chair to officiate could be Lynch himself). The format of the menu is understated: two sheets of folded computer-printed paper inside a laminated cream-colored cover. Clearly, the document is designed to inform, not to upstage.

The menu says nothing about canapés, but there they are. A server, one of several who will visit the table during the evening, brings a silver tray bearing a generous selection of *amuse-gueule*, little nibbles such as curried shrimp on toast squares, parmesan crisps, onion tartlets, and biscuits concealing slivered Virginia ham. Have as many as you want, guests are encouraged. This is the first surprise to emerge from Patrick O'Connell's kitchen. It will not be the last.

Another server brings the bread basket containing crusty rolls and slender slices of country rye with fennel; sourdough; and rye with currants and pecans. A sprig of rosemary garnishes the disk of butter. The breads are delectable, so the plate will be empty before long. But it will not stay empty. The staff has a laserlike ability to spot a bread plate that needs replenishing or a water glass that needs refilling. There is no need to ask. It will be done, and done again, but never when the guest has stepped away. At the Inn, only people, not positions, are served.

By now, the front waiter has extended a welcome, answered the inevitable menu questions, and taken orders for

Guests who stay over learn that the elegant service continues at breakfast.

the first course, the between course, and the main course. The encyclopedic servers are required to know how each dish is prepared and the origin of all its ingredients. Upon bringing a surprise taste of the first Rappahannock County morels of the season, waiter Eric Brass volunteers that the morel season is barely longer than the month of April. Locals call the precious mushroom "merkles," he says, "because it's a miracle if you can find them." Absent from any response at the Inn is the phrase, "I don't know." When a waiter doesn't know the answer to a question, the preferred response is, "Allow me to find out for you." The answer will follow in short order.

All servers are well versed in the Inn's wine program, too, and considerable care is devoted to coordinating the wine service with the evening's menu. With some 1,000 vintages to choose from, distinguishing the subtle differences is a continual challenge for the staff. If additional expertise is required, a server will call on a more experienced member of the team to be at tableside during the selection process and when the bottle is presented for inspection.

Sipping the wine provides an opportunity to scan the softly lit dining room and spy on what others are eating. (Hey, isn't that Newt Gingrich at that corner table?). The well-dressed older couple across the way, who arrived well before, is already into dessert. "Happy Birthday" is drizzled in chocolate around the perimeter of the woman's plate, which holds a mighty pyramid of butter pecan ice cream. Chances are, several other birthdays and anniversaries are being celebrated in the dining room. Someone may even be proposing marriage at this very moment.

A nearby party of four is about to receive the main course. Four waiters glide into the dining room, each bearing a plate at waist level. In unison, the plates are lowered before each diner,

Servers are required to know how each dish is prepared and the origin of all the ingredients.

The Five Stages of Dining

Patrick O'Connell feels strongly that everyone on his staff should be aware of what the guests experience from the moment they call for a reservation until they pay their check. Borrowing a page from psychiatrist Elisabeth Kubler-Ross, who described five stages of dying in her 1969 best-seller *On Death and Dying,* O'Connell has identified the five stages of dining. The stages, which are emblazoned in classical lettering overhead in the kitchen, are:

■ **Anticipation** builds as the guests clip articles about the Inn, make a reservation, and dream about what it will be like to dine at this singular restaurant.

■ **Trepidation** sets in upon arriving at the Inn. There is "a bit of anxiety because their fantasy has finally collided with reality," says O'Connell, "and they are a little apprehensive that it may not live up to everything they imagined it would be."

■ **Inspection.** Only after guests have had a second sip of wine are they relaxed enough to look around at their surroundings and begin to enjoy themselves.

■ **Fulfillment** is a sort of animal sense of sensuality and satiety that occurs upon the second or third bite of the main course. "At this point," O'Connell says, "they are over the main hurdles."

■ **Evaluation** kicks in when the check is presented. "If it's a party of two," says the chef, "the husband will look up and make eye contact with the wife. She might ask, 'How much was it?' He tells her, and she smiles. That means it was all worth it."

touching down simultaneously. The synchronization is breathtaking. How do they *do* that?

The wonderment is interrupted when your server delivers a demitasse of soup. Like the canapés, the soup, which changes nightly according to what ingredients are freshest, isn't listed on the menu.

"Tonight, the chef has prepared a salsify soup," the server says. The velvety white liquid is delicious and earthy. But what on earth is salsify? The Inn at Little Washington had anticipated the question; at the service meeting that afternoon, a definition of salsify (a root vegetable with an oysterlike flavor) was read verbatim from Anne Willen's *La Varenne Pratique, the Complete Illustrated Cooking Course.*

A server visits to crumb the table with a folded napkin. The bread has been restocked; one almost forgets that the bread server had been there, so unobtrusive is the service. The party of four is well into their entrées; they are sampling from each other's plates. Go ahead and ask them what they're having. Food this flawless and imaginative invites comparing notes.

The first course arrives, two plates touching down at exactly the same moment. Talk about art! Each dish is like a canvas. On one is the seared duck foie gras on polenta with country ham and huckleberries; on the other, grilled tandoori quail on curried lentils. As beautiful as the presentation is, it cannot upstage the taste of the food. O'Connell's culinary hallmark is the pristine quality and remarkable freshness of ingredients and the flavors they impart. Those

*Everyone is well versed
in providing service that
is attentive without
being intrusive.*

huckleberries, quite likely, were picked not much more than a day before.

The birthday couple leaves, doubtless convinced that they could not have chosen a more elegant setting for the celebration. More bread arrives. The front waiter, by now an old friend, drops by to ask how everything is. Reinhardt Lynch says hello too. When not chatting with customers, the co-owner can be seen tending to place settings and otherwise overseeing the set. Nothing intrudes on table conversation, however. The background music is low, and the staff go about their business noiselessly, almost invisibly.

The between-course selections are brought: lemon-rosemary sorbet with vermouth and a salad of baby green beans with black truffle vinaigrette. More wine is poured. Before long, the main course arrives with the same theatrical precision. The pan-seared, truffle-dusted Chilean sea bass with shallot fondue, fingerling potatoes, wild mushrooms, and red wine demi glace lives up to every one of its 31 syllables. It is visually astonishing as well, thanks to the deep red puddle of demi glace and the bright green puree of leek.

The other entrée, local rabbit braised in apple cider with wild mushrooms and garlic mashed potatoes, is a perfect example of how O'Connell applies classic French techniques to the preparation of Virginia ingredients. With the first bite, the realization hits: This is why you have traveled many miles to Washington, Virginia.

But the most whimsical part of the evening is still to come. After the dinner plates are cleared, the menus are presented again, this time for dessert. As always, the server is ready for questions. There are certain to be questions

The wine cellar is bound to have
a vintage that will go with any dish.

MAKING SURE GUESTS LEAVE HAPPIER THAN THEY ARRIVED

Unbeknownst to dinner guests, The Inn at Little Washington has their number. The "mood rating" is a mainstay of the Inn's highly regarded service program, a simple tactic that forces the staff to tune in to the emotional state of the customers.

In most cases, the front waiter assigns the initial rating, usually a number between 6 and 9 that is based on his and others' observations about the demeanor of the dining party (10 connotes perfection). The rating is written on the dinner order "dupe," which is attached to a spindle in the kitchen for the entire staff to see.

Sometimes, however, the rating is assigned even before the customers reach the dining room. They might arrive 20 minutes late for a 6 o'clock reservation, complaining of traffic on the Beltway. Or, a couple might enter the Inn with an argument at full throttle.

Upon sensing a problem, whoever greets the party at the door or the reception desk will send word that a 6 ("critical") has arrived. "Once we know that something is going on with a particular guest, it goes through here like wildfire," says Francois LePelch, a dining room service manager.

Patrick O'Connell points out that the procedure is rooted in the Inn's philosophy. "We take responsibility for whatever is happening at a table," he says. "Whether they're worried about a flat tire on the way here or are having a marital dispute, we consider it our problem. Otherwise, how are they going to have a sublime experience?"

The service staff's goal is to ensure that no party leaves the dining room without a rating of 9 or 10. A couple starting with a 9, after being fortified with extraordinary food and wine and cosseted over the course of three hours, is a cinch 10. But a "critical" couple merits heightened attention or, as longtime waiter Eric Brass puts it, "more eyes on the table." They might receive complimentary champagne, a surprise first course, or both, depending on how volatile their mood. One powerful weapon in the Inn's arsenal is a personal invitation from the chef to tour the kitchen, com-

plete with a signed menu. Another is an extra dessert. Whatever it takes.

With so subjective a system, what can stop the waiter writing the dessert order from inflating a table's rating to make himself look good? That will not work, says Brass, "because of the nature of our guests. If someone is unhappy, 99 percent of the time they'll write a letter explaining why, and it would be easy to discover who padded the rating. The seating chart is always saved, so it is known who waited on whom. We are totally accountable here for all our actions."

With the first bite, the realization hits—
This is why you have traveled many
miles to Washington, Virginia.

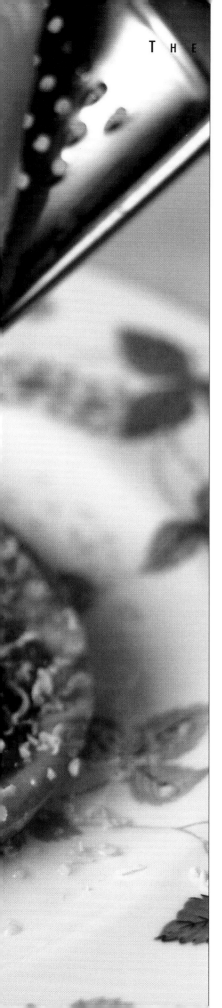

because the tantalizing menu invites them. Just what are the Seven Deadly Sins? And tell us, please, about My Grandmother's Rhubarb Pizza.

Anticipation builds. What has the kitchen wrought this time? Seven Deadly Sins turns out to be a plate of seven bigger-than-bite-sized finishers, more heavenly than deadly, arranged in a circle. There is ice cream, a sorbet, a tart or two, a slab of Valrhona chocolate cake with its molten center, and more.

My Grandmother's Rhubarb Pizza is presented with a fanfare that does honor to chef O'Connell's grandmother, who cultivated rhubarb in her Wisconsin garden. The server identifies the "tomato sauce" (strawberry puree), "green olives" (pistachios), and "black olives" (currants) before grating "parmesan cheese" (white chocolate) over the top and drizzling on the "olive oil" (Galliano). Voilà! Pizza, Little Washington style.

It has been more than three hours since the tray of canapés opened the meal, yet it is still not over. There is coffee, of course, and "for our guests, this final seduction," the waiter says, depositing miniature picnic baskets brimming with chocolates, dime-size cookies, and the candied grapefruit peel introduced to The Inn by an elderly neighbor, Martha Ball Fletcher (*see* Chapter 10).

A final seduction indeed, and one best saved for the next day. Time now, if the guest is lucky, to meet the artist who produced the evening's seductions. Patrick O'Connell's kitchen is a beehive of activity, but the chef usually can break away to extend a hand and thank the visitor for coming all the way to The Inn, his home, for dinner.

Signature dish: The "pizza" that O'Connell named for his grandmother is a popular dessert.

Decor invites guests to come in and relax.

Setting a table is just one art that servers must master.

The Inn at Little Washington

CHAPTER SEVEN

A TEAM ATTUNED TO PERFECTION

It is 5 p.m., and the daily service meeting is in full swing in the dining room. As always, there is much to cover: the breakage report, the day's sales from the gift shop, a demonstration of a new item for the breakfast menu, a review of the number of guests expected that evening, and the birthdays and anniversaries being celebrated. Special note is made of the celebrities. This evening's crop includes a travel writer (make sure her view of the dining room is unobstructed), a famous biographer (the chef is preparing a special menu for her party), and a foreign ambassador (his nation's colors are flying out front).

General manager Scott Little says the hand towels in the men's room are not aligned properly; please see that they are. Patrick O'Connell, his lanky frame folded into a chair, notices that the salmon-hued ginger blossoms flowing from the dining room's signature ceramic swan aren't their freshest. He pulls them out, fluffs the rest of the arrangement, and sends a waiter to fetch new stalks from the florist.

The menus are handed out, changes from the previous night noted, and difficult pronunciations—prosciutto, Sauternes—practiced. All present are then thrust into the role of proofreader. Good thing, too. The second line of a main course selection, "Rockfish Roasted with White Wine, Clams, Shrimp, Mussels, and

"Smile as much as you possibly can," Reinhardt Lynch tells the staff, "especially when things start getting rough."

Everyone on the staff performs tasks to exacting standards.

Black Olives on Toasted Couscous," is off-center. This won't do; the page is imperfect and someone will notice. The menus are hastily gathered up. The line will be fixed on the computer and new pages run off and placed between the laminated covers.

The Inn at Little Washington is about perfection. Everything has to be right: menus, flowers, tablecloths, napkins, towels—the complete guest experience. To make that happen, all employees, especially those who have contact with customers, must do their jobs to perfection. "We are not allowed to have an off night," says Little, who became the Inn's

General manager Scott Little: "We are not allowed to have an off night."

first general manager in 1997. "The organization does not allow it, and our guests are very unforgiving. For some part of our service to fall below the standard, or for a person to make a mistake, is unacceptable. We have to be on all the time. To our servers' credit, they *are* on 99.9 percent of the time."

O'Connell and Reinhardt Lynch set the tone, and their 75 full-time employees—waiters, cooks, housekeepers, telephone reservationists, department heads, administrative assistants, a florist, and a horticulturist—follow through impeccably. Everyone is on the same page; everyone is aware that people come to the Inn with the grandest of expectations; everyone knows it is up to them to fulfill their guests' fantasies and to do so with genuine warmth. "Smile as much as you possibly can," Lynch tells the staff, "especially when things start getting rough."

The Inn hires "almost totally on attitude, and we turn away anyone displaying the slightest hint of haughtiness," O'Connell says. "The simple ingredient is an applicant's overwhelming desire to please people. There are many people in this industry who are without that faculty. They want to be stars. They might have a lot of technical ability, but if they don't want to put their guests first, it's all for naught."

Finding and retaining employees is one of the owners' greatest challenges. At first, they hired from the immediate vicinity, but as the operation grew in complexity and reputation, they cast their net farther and wider. Now, employees come from throughout the United States and overseas. They are required to reside within 30 minutes or so of the Inn, which means they must be able to adapt to rural living.

Most important, employees have to be comfortable working at the Inn, which is demanding of its staff and exceedingly vigilant about the image it portrays to guests and the general public. Even

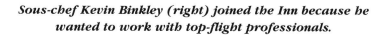

Sous-chef Kevin Binkley (right) joined the Inn because he wanted to work with top-flight professionals.

Everyone knows it is up to them to fulfill their guests' high expectations.

BANISH THE "N" WORD!

On starting at The Inn at Little Washington, the first thing an employee learns is don't say *no*.

"That just seems instinctive," Patrick O'Connell says. "Guests want to be able to feel that any fantasy they have can be addressed. They should have the right to want what they want."

The don't-say-no rule holds even when a request goes against the Inn's grain. Suppose, for example, that a woman asks, "May I have some pickles with my foie gras?" General manager Scott Little says, "We will first say, 'The acidity of the pickles might interfere just slightly with the wonderful buttery consistency of the foie gras.' And if the guest replies, 'That's okay, I like it that way,' we will say, 'Very good, madam,' and we'll go find some pickles to put on it."

Banishing *no* from the staff's lexicon is more than a matter of declining to decline. "We just don't use the word, period," Little says. "If a guest asks, 'Is it spicy?' we won't answer no even if it's as sweet as can be. We will say something like, 'Actually, it's quite a harmonious blend.'"

when walking to their cars at the end of their shift, employees uphold the Inn's high standards—no changing into sneakers and no unbuttoned collars. "The staff are our ambassadors," Lynch says. "They represent Patrick and Reinhardt, and if they don't understand that after a period of time, it is not going to work out."

Once hired, employees undergo a rigorous one-on-one training regimen, which Little describes as "a sort of European apprenticeship in which they start out with the basics and do their job over and over and over again until they do it right." Servers, for example, learn to carry water pitchers, plates, and utensils above the belt. They learn to negotiate the corners when walking through the dining room; to "walk a plate" and set it down silently before a guest.

"We break them of a lot of habits they've learned at other restaurants," Little says, "things like asking the guest if you can have their plate. All you have to say is, 'Finished?' And if you are pouring water into a glass and say 'Pardon my arm,' you are injecting service into the experience of the table unnecessarily. You just do it; you don't talk about it."

Francois LePelch and Neil O'Heir, the senior members of the dining room

After mastering the basics, workers move on to executing the menu's more intricate items.

*Servers must have in-depth
knowledge of food, wine, decor,
and the Inn's traditions.*

staff, take new servers under their wing, training them for several months. The newcomers learn by doing, gradually assuming additional responsibilities. "When I started at the Inn," says LePelch, a Maryland native who has worked in restaurants for more than 20 years, "I served the bread and butter, and once I mastered that I moved up to back waiter. When I was comfortable with that, I took one of the hardest tests in my life."

In this test, veteran members of the dining room staff, playing the roles of inquisitive guests, fire a bewildering array of questions at the prospective waiter. The questions may be about specific menu items, dietary requests, details of the building, wine pairings, local history, even the owners' pet Dalmatians. After passing this test, the server becomes a "full cut" waiter, which means that he or she ascends to the coveted position of front waiter and receives a full cut of the tip pool.

In restaurant circles, working in the kitchen or the dining room at The Inn at Little Washington is a sure sign of arrival. Sous-chef Kevin Binkley, who started his career at 14 in a frozen-yogurt shop and went to the Scottsdale Culinary School in Arizona, wanted to land at the best restaurant possible. "But I never dreamed I would get a job here," says Binkley,

THOSE WHO SERVE DO MORE THAN WAIT

It is not enough to know how to uncork and pour a bottle of wine properly or brush crumbs from a tablecloth. Servers, the Inn's most conspicuous emissaries, are required to be storehouses of knowledge about the place where they earn their living.

To keep them on their toes, general manager Scott Little administers pop quizzes at the daily service meetings. Anything about The Inn at Little Washington's cuisine, history, furnishings, accolades, idiosyncracies, or surroundings is fair game. To wit:

Q: On what page can you find The Inn at Little Washington in the 1999 Relais & Châteaux directory?

A: Page 495.

Q: What's this funny little bug I'm seeing around here?

A: The box elder bug.

Q: When was the Inn built?

A: 1900.

Q: What's special about our Mobil Five-Star rating?

A: The Inn was the first establishment to receive five stars for both its dining room and its lodging.

How seriously the Inn regards this attention to detail may be seen in the exchange that takes place when Little asks a waiter, "Who is depicted in the painting above the goose in the lobby?"

The man hesitates before responding, "Please allow me to check." That is not good enough for Little, who reminds the waiter that the personage is none other than Jean-Anthelme Brillat-Savarin, author of *The Physiology of Taste*.

"That was in the employee newsletter two weeks ago," Little says firmly. "There's no excuse for not knowing." He informs the man that his services won't be needed that evening and suggests that he use the time off to brush up on the Inn's lore.

Later, the general manager explains the rationale for insisting that staff learn everything about the Inn and its operations. "This is the kind of information that everyone needs to commit to memory," he says. "Our guests ask about the Savarin painting all the time, and if we just guess or don't know, it deflates the guest experience."

who scours the globe for ingredients and works closely with O'Connell on developing new menu items. What has he learned from O'Connell? "He has given me an understanding of food," says Binkley, "of how ingredients work together and of the importance of using the best products and keeping them as close to their pure state as possible."

LePelch knows of no better preparation for his dream of having his own restaurant. "It all starts with Chef," he says, referring to O'Connell. "He is my teacher, and he instills in me the feeling that the curtain rises each day for a new show."

Indeed, alumni of the Inn go on to responsible positions in the finest kitchens and dining rooms. Vincent deLouise and Heidi Morf, a husband-and-wife team who own the highly regarded Four & Twenty Blackbirds in nearby Flint Hill, Virginia, are a case in point. They worked separately at the Inn, deLouise as a waiter in the late 1970s and Morf as a chef in the 1980s. The experience was intense—and invaluable.

"The Inn was unlike any place I had ever worked, because Patrick and Reinhardt were perfectionists from the very beginning and wanted and demanded that everything be done right," deLouise says. "It wasn't my favorite place to work, but it was a wonderful place to train."

Daily service meetings cover everything from gift shop sales to the correct pronunciation of new items on the menu.

The Inn at Little Washington

CHAPTER EIGHT

AN OASIS IN THE MIDDLE OF NOWHERE

You never know who will find their way to Patrick and Reinhardt's place in the Shenandoah Valley. Newt Gingrich? Been there. Al and Tipper Gore? Been there, for their anniversary. Barbra Streisand? Been there, for lunch—no easy feat, considering The Inn at Little Washington doesn't serve lunch. But when the White House phoned to say that its house guest, Miss Streisand, wanted to come for lunch the following day, Patrick O'Connell didn't demur. He prepared a special tasting menu for the singer and her friend, who had the dining room to themselves. "Barbra Streisand was very flattering," the chef says. "She told me, 'Your work is exactly like mine: You do more than you have to.'"

Hosting the rich and famous is old hat for O'Connell and Reinhardt Lynch. Political leaders, journalists, movie stars, and titans of industry come to The Inn at Little Washington for the same reason everyone else does: No restaurant makes its guests feel more special and better cared for. What's more, the celebrities need not worry about undue publicity. Washington, Virginia, is far enough from the madding crowd to ensure privacy for those accustomed to seeing their name in the gossip columns, and the Inn's ever-so-discreet employees would never divulge a confidence.

Actor Paul Newman, who has celebrated a birthday or two at the Inn, is a big fan. "When people in Congress feel poorly about their accom-

"When people in Congress feel poorly about their accomplishments, they should go to The Inn at Little Washington for reaffirmation of what is truly good about our country." —*Paul Newman*

plishments," he says, "they should go to The Inn at Little Washington for reaffirmation of what is truly good about our country."

Yet it is just plain folks, not the luminaries of Hollywood and Capitol Hill, who keep the Inn humming along. "We have international travelers and very wealthy people who go to only the finest places," O'Connell says, "but the core of our business is middle-class people who feel comfortable coming here for a special occasion and making the financial sacrifice to do so."

Seventy percent of the Inn's dinner customers and a third of the overnight guests are from the Washington, D.C., area. They plan their visits months, sometimes years, ahead, making their reservations, marking their calendars, counting the days, and then driving an hour or more on unfamiliar roads, expecting to be served a meal they will remember forever.

As one lady proclaimed when she arrived at the front door, "My husband has never in his life driven so far to go out to dinner. If this isn't the best meal he's ever had, he is going to kill me!" Observes O'Connell, "That is the kind of pressure they bring with them."

Like all restaurants, The Inn at Little Washington has its regulars. Eugene McCarthy, the former senator from Minnesota who sought the presidency in 1968, lives in Rappahannock County and comes for dinner every so often, "when I get tired of my own cooking." He crosses his fingers and hopes the chef has trout on the menu.

The Nelsons of Great Falls, Virginia, like the trout, too, and everything else they have tasted at the Inn, which is a lot. Marti, a radiologist, and Wayne, a stockbroker, hold the Inn's unofficial record for most dinners

A quiet corner (opposite) offers solitude. Above, fresh berries remind patrons that the Inn's produce comes right from the land.

Just the Place for a Quiet Little Wedding

Even by Big Washington standards, the 100 people who came to Washington, Virginia, on April 6, 1997, made for an awesome assemblage of prestige and power. On that Sunday afternoon, NBC White House correspondent Andrea Mitchell and Federal Reserve Chairman Alan Greenspan were married in the Inn's courtyard garden, which was just beginning to show its springtime colors.

"As one of our waiters said, every diner at his station had been on the cover of either *Newsweek* or *Time*," says Patrick O'Connell, himself bowled over by a guest list that included Henry Kissinger, Colin Powell, and such TV newsroom habitués as Barbara Walters, Sam Donaldson, and Tim Russert. "To see that many very famous people in one place was one of those filmlike feelings."

Seldom had the Inn seen such a display of celebrity. "There wasn't anyone there who wasn't well known," says O'Connell. "I was walking by our side door and saw two men helping a little lady out of the back of a car and into the kitchen. I couldn't imagine what they were doing. It turned out to be Supreme Court Justice Ruth Bader Ginsburg, who was going to officiate at the ceremony. There had been too many reporters out front, so she decided to slip in through the back."

For Reinhardt Lynch the event was a milestone in the Inn's history. "Having that wedding here," he says, "was a reaffirmation that we have done something right, something good, something the world can acknowledge."

But O'Connell and Lynch and their staff had precious little time to bask in the glow or pinch themselves at having been in the company of so many movers and shakers. As soon as the newlyweds and their famous friends departed for the Beltway, there were still more dignitaries to prepare for: that evening's dinner guests.

*The attentive waitstaff has
proved a prime factor in bringing
the Inn worldwide recognition.*

consumed there—somewhere between 150 and 200. They don't wait for a special occasion. Every two months or so they can be found at their favorite table against the wall in the main dining room. Sometimes, at the owners' invitation, they have dessert in the kitchen. "It's theater—like going to the Kennedy Center for one of the great plays," Wayne says. "Everything is happening around you."

The Nelsons remember their first visit more than 20 years ago. They came with a friend who had heard about a wonderful little restaurant in the middle of nowhere. Reinhardt Lynch was greeting customers at the door, the reception area was bare concrete, and a ceramic dog rested nearby. The party feasted on smoked trout served with pickles and sliced cucumbers, sour cream, and horseradish, as well as timbale of crab and spinach under a glass dome. "We tried it, we loved it, and we decided to come back as often as possible," Marti says.

The proprietors and the Nelsons occasionally break bread together, but away from the Inn. Nevertheless, "the Inn is what Patrick and Reinhardt always talk about," Wayne says, offering an insight into why things proceed flawlessly there. "It is the only thing on their minds, so you can understand why it's so great."

Customers obviously keep the spot in mind when marking personal milestones. The Inn has had a hand in thousands of marriage proposals and even a smattering of divorces. "There was a couple I'd chatted with over the years, and they came back for dinner and said this would be their last time at the Inn," Lynch recalls. "I asked if they were moving away, and they said, no, they'd just been divorced, and this would be their last meal together. It's like we meant so much to them that even after their divorce they would bother to get together and come here! It takes your breath away."

Although Lynch and O'Connell do not claim to be experts in snuffing out romance, they do have the marriage proposal down to an art form. Hardly a

"The Inn is what Patrick and Reinhardt always talk about. It is the only thing on their minds, so you can understand why it's so great." —*Wayne Nelson, a longtime customer*

THE NIGHT FRANCOIS SAVED THE DAY

It is a tribute to O'Connell and Lynch and their staff that customers invariably have an "Inn story" to share. Candida Sampson's tale, about how the Inn handled a delicate moment, speaks volumes about the Inn's special bond with its customers.

Sampson, an executive from Washington, D.C., and her boyfriend had completed a romantic dinner and were about to hit the road. Her boyfriend reached into his jacket pocket for his wallet. It wasn't there. "I haven't got my wallet," he said.

Sampson started laughing because she thought he was kidding. "We'd just had a $400 dinner!"

"Honey, I'm not kidding. I don't have my wallet!" He went out to the car, but a frantic search turned up nothing. He returned dripping wet. It had started to rain.

"I'd taken this tiny evening bag and I didn't have my credit cards," Sampson recalls vividly. "Here we are, in one of the most prestigious restaurants in the world, and he forgot his wallet!"

Mortified, she stormed out of the restaurant, leaving her distraught companion to deal with the Inn. "You're on your own," she informed him.

As Sampson simmered in the car, her boyfriend explained his predicament to Francois LePelch, one of the Inn's dining room service managers. Unbeknownst to Sampson, her boyfriend had earlier made a reservation for another dinner as a birthday surprise. No problem, Francois said. The Inn could look up that reservation and get the credit card number, or the bill could be paid by mail.

Francois had a more pressing concern, howev-

Francois LePelch

er: Sampson's frazzled state. He had seen her leave, obviously upset. So he grabbed an umbrella, and the next thing he was outside in the rain knocking on the car window.

"Madam, please come back," he pleaded. "We just feel awful about this." Sampson got out of the car. "You know, madam, this happens all the time," Francois continued. "This is not a problem."

He guided her back into the restaurant and gave the couple a private space off the reception area. He brought a brandy and said, "Spend some time with the gentleman and don't worry about anything." A while later, he was back with an enormous basket of petits fours and a posy of flowers. "It's *really* not a problem, madam," he said again. "We want you to have good memories of your first visit here. Please don't be upset with the gentleman."

Crisis averted, relationship saved, the couple thanked Francois and went out to the car. Sampson's boyfriend immediately stepped on his wallet, which was immersed in a puddle.

What to do now? "I felt terrible," Sampson says, "but I got my boyfriend to go back in there and tell Francois what had happened. He showed him the wallet, which was dripping wet, and offered to pay the bill. And all Francois said was, 'You have more important things to take care of.' It was the most embarrassing thing that ever happened to us, and this man could not have been more gracious."

Two months later, on her birthday, Sampson and her boyfriend were back for another sumptuous meal at the Inn, his wallet safely ensconced in her evening bag.

week passes without an engagement ring being secreted in a bowl of cherries, a plate of oysters, or one of the kitchen's most popular creations, a caramel cage. For those craving even more originality, the Inn rolls out various props, such as a music box with a snow scene and a mouse that dances on a tiny mirror. The mouse wears the engagement ring on a gold chain around its neck.

Chris Currie, a public relations supervisor from Hyattsville, Maryland, chose another ring-bearing option when he reserved a table for the biggest dinner of his life, for popping the question to journalist Susie Powell. "I told the reservationist I was going to propose marriage and that I didn't want the ring to be obvious. I also said I didn't want the waiter there, because I was nervous enough as it was. The lady on the phone suggested that the ring be placed on a little dish covered in rose petals."

Currie and Powell drove to the Inn on a Saturday night during the Christmas season in 1996. Because Susie's birthday was a few days away, she thought the dinner was meant to celebrate that. So far so good. The couple was seated in a corner of the Terrace Room overlooking the courtyard and, to ensure privacy, the adjacent table was left empty. Perfect. Before long, though, Currie realized he had a problem: He had forgotten to slip the ring to the headwaiter.

"I started looking for an excuse to leave the table, and then Susie sneezed, so I told her I was going to get her a tissue," he recalls. "I jumped up and as soon as I left the room, someone grabbed me and whisked me away to another man. This guy took me to a third man, who said, 'Oh, Mr. Currie, we understand you have a very special evening planned. Let's go over the details.' It happened so fast I felt like I was being abducted." He handed over the ring, obtained a tissue, and returned to the table. Mission accomplished.

After lingering over a delicious meal, the couple ordered dessert. A waiter brought over a heart-shaped, petal-strewn plate and announced, "We have a special dessert for you, ma'am." He placed it in front of Powell and faded away, at which point Currie knelt before his future wife and proposed.

Proposal accepted, the couple received an extra dessert and champagne compliments of the Inn, and a surprise visit from chef O'Connell. On the way out, there were congratulations from the dining room staff as well.

"I can't imagine a more perfect way to get engaged," says the new Mrs. Currie. And her husband will never forget the night he was abducted by a team of well-meaning—and highly efficient—waiters just doing their job at The Inn at Little Washington.

Hardly a week passes without an engagement ring being secreted in a bowl of cherries, a plate of oysters, or one of the kitchen's most popular creations, a caramel cage.

The Inn at Little Washington

CHAPTER NINE

A Place Where the Critics Run Out of Superlatives

Barely two months after Patrick O'Connell and Reinhardt Lynch started serving customers at the crossroads they call Little Washington, Big Washington's afternoon paper blew their cover. "Once in a great while there comes a restaurant so good that you worry," *Washington Star* dining columnist John Rosson wrote in the April 2, 1978, edition. "You ask yourself: Was everything that happened a series of fortunate flukes? Or, if it's that good, will it crumble under the pressure of success?"

Rosson went on to swoon over the "melt in your mouth" bread and herb-infused butter, the "refined" watercress soup, and the "marvelously light" *mousse de foie de canard* topped with duck aspic and served in a tiny crock. Moving on to dessert, he wrote, "I have not seen more beautiful tarts in years," and singled out the pear tart interlaced with almond cream and "given a dash of color by way of prunes." Rosson anointed The Inn at Little Washington one of the finest restaurants within 150 miles of the nation's capital. The stampede was on.

Three months later, the *Washington Post*'s Phyllis Richman offered her first impressions. "Washington finally has a first-rate French restaurant," Richman wrote, stretching the city limits to include the Blue Ridge foothills. The freshness of the food and the "city-country" balance of the menu captivated Richman, though she also noted lapses: an overly sauced veal dish here, insufficiently browned puff pastry cases there. "But," she continued

Garden sorrel vichyssoise (opposite) is one reason food writers rave about the Inn's fare.

forgivingly, "one is hard-pressed to remember such flaws in a meal that wends its way from homemade breads with herbed butter through aspic-glazed mousse of duck to impeccable soft-shell crabs and pastries so stunning that you order them all."

From the beginning, dining critics and food writers have groped for the superlatives to describe dinner at the Inn, their raves playing neatly into the partners' time-honored marketing strategy: Don't spend a dime on advertising when glowing reviews and word of mouth will do.

Five years passed before word of the Inn's excellence spread beyond the Beltway. In the spring of 1983, *The New York Times*'s Marian Burros noted "the unexpected combinations of ingredients" that O'Connell somehow made work: baked mussels with fennel and red bell pepper, a timbale of crabmeat and spinach mousse. The Inn, she wrote, "was on a par with New York's best restaurants and more inventive than most of them." Not long afterward, her globetrotting colleague Craig Claiborne remarked, "I had the most fantastic meal of my life here."

A decade later, accolades were still pouring in. Composer Andrew Lloyd Webber, in his "Matters of Taste" column in *The Daily Telegraph* of London, called dinner at the Inn "the best overall dining experience I can remember in a long while, perhaps my best ever." To John Mariani, prolific dining critic and author, The Inn at Little Washington is "exactly the kind of restaurant I most love, because the owners work their hardest and have their signature on it."

The enthusiastic notices are not limited to newspa-

Imposing words lettered above them remind kitchen workers of the high standards that have won them acclaim.

The Inn's reputation for impeccable service can be traced to training sessions like this.

per and magazine dining columns. An exclusive overnight destination, the Inn has received copious coverage in travel magazines and newspaper travel sections. "A 10-star property, can you believe it?" the *Dallas Morning News* marveled, awarding five stars for the food and five for the accommodations.

Rosson, now retired, and Phyllis Richman still make the epicurean pilgrimage to Rappahannock County. Neither has grown tired of it. "It just gets better and better," says Richman, who has spent a birthday or two in thrall in the dining room. Except for the occasional too-sweet entrée and the owners' penchant for frilly lampshades, the veteran dining critic finds little to fault. "I never liked their lampshades," she says. "They changed them, and I don't like the new ones either. But there is nothing tortured about the food."

Dinner at the Inn has special appeal for Rosson, who grew up on a farm in neighboring Culpeper County. As a child, he and his brother collected aromatic sassafras bark and brewed it into tea. O'Connell has his own use for local sassafras: He turns it into a delicate, pale-pink, between-course granita. "And his trout is from a river two

"I had the most fantastic meal of my life here."
—*Craig Claiborne*

At the Top of Zagat's List

Olga Boikess has a tough job. As editor of the Washington, D.C./Baltimore *Zagat Survey,* Boikess distills diners' comments into the pithy, 50-word capsules for which the Zagat guides are famous. The Inn at Little Washington, the highest-rated restaurant in the history of the *Zagat Survey,* provides Boikess with lots of material to work with, maybe too much. After all, how can one write a fresh capsule every two years when the same old superlatives tumble forth?

For the 1999 survey, 592 of the 3,750 Washington/Baltimore respondents had dined at the Inn, a phenomenal percentage considering the price tag and the difficulty of landing a table. "There are just pages and pages that start, 'The best . . .'," Boikess says. Other reiterated phrases include "spectacular," "opulent," "magical service," "attention to detail," "nearly perfect," "worth every penny," "nirvana," and "heaven." Boikess's favorite comment, perhaps from a romantic linguist: "The place to propose marriage or consummate vowels."

The Inn at Little Washington was first rated by Zagat in 1988, scoring a 28 (out of 30) for food and a 27 for both decor and service. Boikess's bare-bones summary that year began by noting the Inn's proximity to the nation's capital. In 1989, O'Connell and Lynch snagged straight 28s and more colorful comments: "the ultimate," "hire a limo." The restaurant racked up straight 29s in 1991, slipped a point in service in 1993, slipped a point in decor in 1995, regained straight 29s in 1997, and maintained its 29s in 1999. No other restaurant has matched the Inn's glittering 29-29-29 record, which is tantamount to perfection because Zagat no longer awards 30s.

Tim Zagat, publisher of the *Zagat Survey,* has his own adjectives to describe his first visit to the Inn with his wife, Nina. "I don't remember the specific meal, other than that it was spectacular; and the breakfast the next morning was mind-boggling—the most fantastic hot popovers and cakes, one thing after another."

But for Zagat, the most vivid memory is of entering their guest room and Nina's screaming, "Oh my God!" On a nightstand by the bed was a silver-framed picture of the couple. "Years later, I'm still telling people how they obtained a picture of Nina and me to make us feel at home," Zagat says. "Those little extra things knock your socks off."

Around the Inn, 29-29-29 is not only a source of great pride but a daily reminder that there are stratospheric expectations to live up to. What if the Inn were to slip from the top rung and receive, say, mere 28s?

"I don't know if I would fall on my knife, but I would certainly feel like it," says O'Connell. "Of course, you would whip yourself and the staff with branches of poison nettles and sleep on a bed of nails for six weeks or so and work extra hard to turn it around."

or three counties up," Rosson says wistfully. "In September, October, and November the apples he uses are from an orchard you can skip to. The cooking is marvelously, seasonally Virginia."

For the young owners, Rosson's 1978 review may have been the first sign that they were onto something. Rosson recalls vivid details from several visits he made to the Inn early that year: the warm greeting from Lynch at the front door, the fresh flowers in the men's room, the dressy curtains and tablecloths, and the local women who brought handfuls of homegrown herbs to the back door. He also considered the dinner a great bargain; the most expensive entrée, the tournedos, was

Critics have high praise for how O'Connell infuses his cuisine with local produce.

$8.95. "It was clear from the start that the quality was near spectacular, especially for a long-neglected rural area," he says.

On the visit just before his review went to print, Rosson introduced himself to O'Connell and Lynch, who already had figured out who he was. "I told them, 'You know, I'm going to write a column and I'm not going to tell you what it'll say, but you'd better watch out because you're going to get jam-packed in here. You're giving your food away.'"

Lynch remembers the conversation too. "What Rosson said was, 'You're going to have to hire a person just to answer the phone.' We thought he was kidding. Everyone here was either serving or cooking food. The thought of hiring someone just to answer the phone seemed like nonsense." Rosson's review came out, and the telephone started ringing. The Inn's next hire was a reservationist. Now, four reservationists are answering phones at any given time.

Significantly, that original *Washington Star* review, so pivotal to the Inn's early success, hangs in a nondescript office out of public view. None of the glowing newspaper or magazine reviews, none of the glittering accolades and awards handed to O'Connell and Lynch by their peers, are displayed in places frequented by guests. The proprietors want people to feel as if they are at a friend's

Because it is off the beaten track,
the innkeepers thought it would take time
for critics to discover their place.
They were wrong.

grand country home, and so the words of dining critics are not framed for all to see.

That does not mean what the critics have to say is unimportant. Past adulation aside, O'Connell acknowledges that anticipating the next review is always nerve-jangling. "You regularly collide with the reality of something someone is going to write," the chef says. "You worry about the unraveling, the undoing of everything you have built up, and the more you have built up, the more you worry about it crumbling. While the public thinks of the Inn as an institutional legend, you are continually reminded of how fragile that legend is."

Being in the country makes it easy to provide guests with home-grown food and fresh herbs and flowers.

"It was clear from the start that the quality was near spectacular." —*John Rosson*

The Inn has brought change to a quiet corner of Virginia.

The Inn at Little Washington

CHAPTER TEN

ONE TOWN'S TAKE ON FAME AND FORTUNE

Most great restaurants are landmarks in their respective communities, but not the *only* landmark. Take away La Grenouille from midtown Manhattan, for example, and the gourmands will get by quite well with Le Bernardin, the Café des Artistes, or '21' Club, all just a New York minute away.

The Inn at Little Washington is different. It is the dominant economic force in a hamlet of 180 people, not many more than the 160 guests Patrick O'Connell's kitchen feeds on a busy night. Because of the Inn, people who had no inkling there was another Washington 65 miles west of the White House pass up Big Washington for no reason other than to stick a fork in some heavenly foie gras. To say the Inn has become the town's raison d'être is not stretching the truth.

Perhaps inevitably, this has resulted in a complicated relationship between the Inn and the community. The town is dependent on the Inn, but some locals resent their world-famous neighbor and the changes it has brought to what was once a quiet, unremarkable county seat. They have little in com-

The town is dependent on the Inn, but some locals resent the changes it has brought, including limousines and the occasional helicopter that deposits well-heeled guests there.

mon with the well-heeled guests deposited on the Inn's doorstep by stretch limousines and the occasional helicopter. In 1999, two decades' worth of uneasiness bubbled over in a most public way when *The New Yorker* vividly reported on the strains.

There are people in and around Washington, Virginia, who never patronize the culinary jewel in their backyard, declaring it not their cup of tea and beyond the reach of their pocketbooks, besides. "The innkeepers wanted to make it as elegant as the places they visited in Europe, and they made it into something that is unfamiliar to people who grew up out here in the country," says Cathryn Knuepfer, a longtime resident and director of the Rappahannock Historical Society.

Adds Norman Getsinger, a retired foreign service officer who lives in nearby Flint Hill, "Some people don't like so much putting on the dog. As long as the Inn goes its way, the town goes its way, and the two don't collide, it's a nice, symbiotic relationship."

To be sure, the Inn contributes much to the town and to Rappahannock County, with 7,000 residents one of the smallest in Virginia. Through the 2.5 percent local meals and lodging tax paid by guests, the Inn accounts for three-quarters of the town's budget. It is the second-largest private employer

Sweet Treat from a Friend Around the Corner

Martha Ball Fletcher, a descendant of George Washington's mother, Mary, had a thing or two to teach The Inn at Little Washington: what to do with the rinds after the breakfast grapefruit juice was pressed.

The grande dame of Washington, Virginia, lived around the corner from the Inn and would bring herbs from her garden to the kitchen door. "Like many of the older women in the community, she was thrilled we were here," Patrick O'Connell says. "In the early days, the ladies would walk by the front windows and look in at the swan and the flowers floating above the dining room. They were so pleased to have a little culture and refinement right in their midst, where life had been a bit like Dodge City before."

The elderly neighbor suggested a use for the grapefruit rinds the kitchen staff were discarding. "She showed us how to make them into candy," O'Connell recalls fondly. "It's not a secret, really. You boil the rind in a simple sugar syrup and dry it. It's the perfect little thing with coffee or tea after a rich meal."

Mattie, as everyone called her, was famous locally for her ham biscuits and homemade pickles, but her days by the stove ended around the time of her hundredth birthday, when she dozed off while frying bacon. It turned out to be a fortuitous mishap. For the rest of her life, the staff at the Inn brought her a noonday meal on a silver tray, flowers included.

In 1996, Martha Ball Fletcher died at age 107. Per her wishes, her friends the innkeepers were her pallbearers. To this day, candied grapefruit rind, served with chocolates after dessert, is a staple of The Inn at Little Washington.

In true Southern tradition, the Inn goes all out to pamper its guests.

Every morning, residents help themselves to the Inn's dinner rolls from a basket in the redbrick post office.

in the county, after the national catalog retailer Faith Mountain Company.

The Inn buys produce and herbs from nearby growers, and hams, rabbit, venison, and other meat products from area purveyors. It hires local contractors and artisans for its construction projects. And it has created a modest local tourism industry. Dinner guests help fill the cash registers of the town's smattering of art galleries and antiques and craft shops. They also are a boon to the five bed-and-breakfasts in town. Overnight rates at the B&Bs are typically less than half those charged by the Inn, which start at $340.

The Inn is an integral part of the social fabric of Washington, Virginia. Every morning, residents help themselves to the Inn's dinner rolls from a basket in the redbrick post office. Many townsfolk have enjoyed the Inn's hospitality at the annual Christmas party. Reinhardt Lynch, who sits on the Town Council, and O'Connell regularly support community fund-raisers by contributing dinners as prizes.

Yet despite these good intentions, O'Connell and Lynch have endured considerable friction since establishing their business. Some townsfolk believe the Inn, which has built a small real estate empire of 17 properties, is acquiring too much control. The innkeepers' development ambitions also have been a source of concern. In 1990, they announced plans for a Tudor-style expansion with 18 guest suites, meeting space, and an indoor pool. The opposition was immediate and vocal; critics maintained the castlelike build-

■

Despite controversy over their expansion plans, O'Connell and Lynch make a point of being part of the community.

ing would stick out amid the brick and clapboard. The proposal was defeated, and it would be another seven years before O'Connell and Lynch completed a scaled-back expansion encompassing the new kitchen and the two guest suites above it.

"Every once in a while, there is a sign that the owners of the Inn lose sight of the fact that they are in a historic, traditional place," Knuepfer says. "Sometimes the Inn comes on a little strong with the things they want to do in town, and we have to ask them to please be a little careful."

O'Connell is philosophical about the Inn's scrapes, saying they come with the territory. Washington, Virginia, after all, is the type of place where everyone knows everyone else, not to mention everyone else's business. Had he and Lynch anticipated this? "We had a sense of the local mentality but perhaps misunderstood how threatening to people significant change can be," he says. "Anyone introducing change in a small landscape is going to be suspiciously regarded. We're always going to have a few diehards talking about the good old days when this was a gas station."

Buying meat and produce from nearby farms has made the Inn an integral part of the local economy.

IMPRESSING THE BEST

Customers and restaurant critics aren't the only ones fumbling for superlatives to describe what Patrick O'Connell and Reinhardt Lynch have wrought. Industry colleagues are wowed, too, even those who haven't found their way to Rappahannock County.

Drew Nieporent has yet to visit The Inn at Little Washington, but he says O'Connell and Lynch's formula is worthy of emulation. "They are raising the bar in terms of their own standards and demanding excellence from themselves and from their staff," says the force behind such renowned restaurants as Montrachet and Nobu in New York City. "It's really a personal place, and it shows the rest of us that you can achieve something on a high plane, take great pride in what you do, and make some money at the same time."

To Warner LeRoy, whose glittering Tavern on the Green is a New York City landmark, the Inn served up "the best overall experience I have had in a restaurant in America. The food is fabulous, the wines are fabulous, the atmosphere is fabulous, and the attention to detail is extraordinary."

Colleagues have recognized O'Connell and Lynch with an armful of James Beard Foundation Awards, the restaurant industry's Oscars. Showing the breadth of its expertise, the Inn has taken home the awards for Outstanding Wine Service, Outstanding Service, and Outstanding Restaurant. O'Connell has won the award for Best Chef—Mid-Atlantic.

No less a legend than Alice Waters, owner of Chez Panisse in Berkeley, California, marvels at the "unheard of" guest experience provided by the Inn. "It's like stepping into a cloud and being taken away," says Waters, considered by many to be the mother of California cuisine. "It's all about understanding people's needs and desires and the little things that make them feel taken care of. It could be the beautiful champagne or those wonderful little nuts that elves must have left in your room. When I stayed overnight, there were pictures of me in my room and books I've written. You don't know where it's all coming from. It appears so effortless, but you know it isn't."

In the dining room, Waters must have been reminded of her own Chez Panisse, where the menu is improvised according to what is freshest that day. Although The Inn at Little Washington is more formal than Chez Panisse and its cooking more influenced by the French school, Waters recognizes similarities between it and the groundbreaking restaurant she started in 1971. Both restaurants "take care of people so that they are very happy when they leave," she says, noting that both have also forged critical relationships with nearby farmers. "A lot of Patrick's food has the sense of being just picked, a sense of being alive."

Marcel Desaulniers, a nationally known cookbook author and chef who owns the Trellis Restaurant in Williamsburg, Virginia, has followed the Inn at Little Washington from the relatively short distance of 150 miles. "There was no doubt that in regard to food and presentation, there was something special going on there," Desaulniers says of his first meal at the Inn, in 1979. "It says something about Patrick and Reinhardt that they didn't start on a big budget or in an area in proximity to much of anything. It's pretty tough to get people to drive 70 miles to your restaurant, but they made it by dint of their talent."

Staying at the Inn, says Alice Waters, "is like stepping into a cloud and being taken away."

The Inn at Little Washington

CHAPTER ELEVEN

RECIPES FROM THE INN AT LITTLE WASHINGTON

Fresh ingredients are a mainstay of the Inn's fare.
Above, a tempting selection of cheeses.

137

Chilled Grilled Black Mission Figs with Virginia Country Ham and Lime Cream

(A cold first course)

Serves 4

12 fresh Black Mission figs,
　sliced in half lengthwise

2 tablespoons olive oil

1 tablespoon sugar

1 teaspoon ground cinnamon

1/2 cup heavy cream

1/4 cup fresh lime juice

Pinch of freshly grated nutmeg

2 limes

6 ounces thinly sliced Virginia
　country ham

4 teaspoons snipped fresh chives
　(optional)

1. Brush the figs with the olive oil.

2. In a small bowl, combine the sugar and cinnamon and sprinkle over the figs.

3. Preheat the gas grill or broiler. If using a grill, lay the figs, flat side down, on the grill rack and heat for 2 to 3 minutes or until they soften but still hold their shape. If using a broiler, place the figs, flat side up, on a lightly oiled baking sheet. Broil the figs as close to the heating element as possible for 2 to 3 minutes. Remove from the heat and let cool to room temperature. (The figs may be prepared a day in advance and kept refrigerated, but their flavor is far superior when they are served at room temperature.)

4. In the bowl of an electric mixer, whip the cream just until it begins to form soft peaks. Slowly add the lime juice and nutmeg. This mixture should have the consistency of a thick sauce. Place the cream in a pastry bag fitted with a plain tip or in a plastic squeeze bottle and refrigerate.

To serve:

1. Cut the limes in half. Slice a bit off the bottom of each lime half so that it will stand upright. Place one lime half in the center of each of four plates.

2. Arrange six of the fig slices around each lime. Loosely drape the ham over the figs. Pipe or squeeze the lime cream over the figs and ham in a thin, lacy pattern. If desired, sprinkle each plate with 1 teaspoon of chives.

Note: This dish may be assembled ahead of time except for the lime cream, which can be made separately, refrigerated, and added just before serving.

Crispy Seared Foie Gras on Polenta with Country Ham and Blackberries

(A hot first course)
Serves 8

Sauce

1 tablespoon butter	1/2 cup cassis
1 tablespoon chopped shallot	2 tablespoons currant jelly
1/2 bay leaf	2 tablespoons chicken stock
1 cup fresh blackberries	1/2 teaspoon finely chopped fresh thyme
1/2 cup water	Freshly ground pepper to taste

Polenta

1 tablespoon butter	1/2 cup heavy cream
4 tablespoons olive oil	1/4 cup yellow cornmeal
1/2 teaspoon minced garlic	1/4 cup freshly grated Parmesan or Asiago cheese
1 bay leaf	Salt and cayenne pepper to taste
1/2 cup water	
1/2 cup milk	

Foie gras

1 foie gras, about 1 1/4 pounds	1 pint fresh blackberries
Salt and freshly ground pepper to taste	

Other ingredients

2 cups mixed greens, such as watercress, frisée, or red oak lettuce	8 very thin slices country ham, trimmed of fat and cut into 2-inch squares
Extra-virgin olive oil	2 tablespoons chopped fresh chives

To make the sauce:

1. In a 2-quart saucepan, melt the butter over low heat. Add the shallot, bay leaf, and blackberries and sweat for 3 minutes.

2. Add the water, cassis, jelly, and stock. Simmer over medium heat for about 30 minutes or until the sauce is the consistency of a light syrup.

3. Remove from the heat and add the thyme and pepper. Set aside for 10 minutes. Strain.

To make the polenta:

1. In a four-quart saucepan, melt the butter over low heat. Add 1 tablespoon of the oil, the garlic, and bay leaf and sweat for 30 seconds.

2. Add the water, milk, and cream and bring to a simmer. Remove the bay leaf.

3. Whisking constantly, add the cornmeal. Simmer for 2 minutes or until the polenta begins to thicken.

4. Whisk in the cheese and season with salt and cayenne.

5. Line a baking sheet with plastic wrap and pour the polenta onto the sheet. Cover with plastic wrap and flatten to about 1/2-inch thick. Refrigerate for 1 hour.

6. Remove from the refrigerator and cut into 2-inch squares. Sauté both sides in the remaining oil until golden brown. Keep warm.

To prepare the foie gras:

1. Soak the foie gras in a bowl of ice water for 10 minutes to draw out the blood and firm up the flesh.

2. Separate the two lobes of the liver, removing any fat or sinew.

3. Using a very sharp knife dipped in warm water, slice the liver on the bias into 1/4-inch slices. Season with salt and pepper.

4. In a heavy skillet, sear the foie gras over high heat for about 30 seconds on each side, or just until a golden brown crust forms. Remove from the skillet and blot on paper towels.

5. Pour off the excess fat and deglaze the pan with the reserved blackberry sauce. Add the fresh blackberries and reduce the sauce to a syrupy consistency.

To serve:

1. In a medium-sized bowl, toss the greens with the oil and salt and pepper. Place a small bouquet of dressed greens in the center of each of eight warm serving plates.

2. Place a square of polenta on top of the greens, then place a slice of ham on top of the polenta. Top with one piece of foie gras.

3. Spoon the sauce over the liver. Sprinkle with the chives.

Our Garden Sorrel Vichyssoise

Serves 6

1/2 cup (1/2 stick) lightly salted
   butter

1 medium onion, coarsely chopped

3 leeks, chopped

3 medium Idaho potatoes, peeled
   and diced

2 bay leaves

2 quarts chicken stock

1 cup fresh sorrel leaves, stemmed
   and chopped

1 tablespoon fresh lemon juice

1/8 cup red wine vinegar

2 cups heavy cream

Salt and white pepper to taste

2 tablespoons chopped fresh
   chives

1. In a 4-quart heavy-bottomed saucepan, melt the butter over medium heat. Add the onion and leeks and cook until tender but not browned (about 7 minutes).

2. Add the potato and bay leaves and cook for 5 minutes.

3. Meanwhile, in a separate saucepan, heat the stock to a boil. Pour the boiling stock over the vegetables. Simmer until the potato is soft (about 15 minutes).

4. Remove the soup from the heat and puree in small batches in a blender or food processor. Strain. Chill in the refrigerator.

5. When the soup is thoroughly chilled, add the sorrel and puree again in a blender or food processor.

6. Transfer the soup to a bowl and whisk in the lemon juice and vinegar. Add the cream. Season with salt and white pepper. Chill thoroughly in the refrigerator.

To serve:

Pour the chilled soup into bowls and sprinkle with chives.

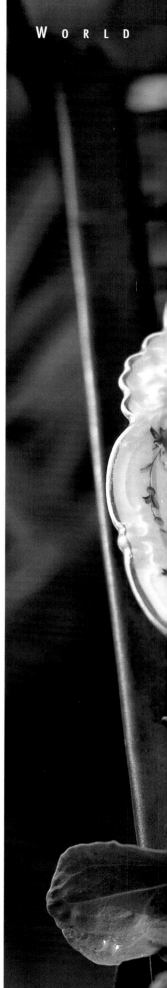

Sweet Red Bell Pepper Soup with Sambuca Cream

Serves 6

1/2 cup olive oil

1 cup chopped onion

1 tablespoon dried fennel seed

1/4 teaspoon dried thyme

1/2 bay leaf, crumbled

1/2 teaspoon minced garlic

1 tablespoon chopped fresh basil
    or 1/2 teaspoon dried

2 tablespoons minced jalapeño
    pepper

1/4 cup all-purpose flour

5 cups chicken stock

1/2 cup peeled, seeded, and
    chopped fresh or canned tomato

1 teaspoon tomato paste

6 large red bell peppers, halved,
    seeded, and cut into 2-inch chunks

1/2 to 1 cup heavy cream

Pinch of sugar

Salt and freshly ground pepper
    to taste

Generous splash of sambuca

Sambuca Cream (*see* recipe opposite)

1. In a 4-quart heavy-bottomed saucepan, heat the 1/2-cup olive oil over medium heat. Add the onion, fennel seed, thyme, bay leaf, garlic, basil, and jalapeño pepper. Reduce the heat to low and cook until the onion is translucent (about 10 to 15 minutes).

2. Add the flour and cook, stirring constantly, for 10 minutes.

3. In a separate pot, bring the stock to a boil. Carefully pour the stock over the vegetables, stirring well to incorporate. Add the tomato and tomato paste.

4. Meanwhile, place a large skillet lightly coated with olive oil over high heat. Sauté the bell pepper chunks until the skins are blistered and lightly charred. Add the peppers to the soup and simmer for about 20 minutes, stirring occasionally to ensure that nothing sticks to the bottom of the pot.

5. Remove the soup from the heat and puree in small batches in a blender or food processor fitted with a steel blade. Strain.

6. Return the soup to the saucepan, bring to a simmer, and add 1/2 cup of the cream and the pinch of sugar. Season with salt and pepper. If the soup is too spicy, add more cream. Add the sambuca just before serving.

To serve:

Serve the soup in individual bowls with a dollop of Sambuca Cream.

Sambuca Cream

Makes 1 cup

1 cup heavy cream

1/2 teaspoon fresh lemon juice

1/4 teaspoon grated lemon zest

3 tablespoons sambuca

Pinch of sugar

In the bowl of an electric mixer, whip the cream until soft peaks form. Add the lemon juice and zest, sambuca, and sugar. Continue whipping until the cream is almost stiff. Keep refrigerated until serving time.

Garden Tomato Salad with Grilled Red Onions, Fresh Basil, and Asiago Cheese

Serves 4 to 6

1/2 cup red wine vinegar

6 sprigs fresh basil

1/2 cup pine nuts

1 bunch watercress

4 ripe garden tomatoes

2 red onions

Salt and cracked black pepper to taste

1/4 cup or more of extra-virgin olive oil

One 8-ounce wedge Asiago cheese

1/2 cup vinaigrette

Sugar to taste

Fresh basil leaves

1. In a small saucepan, bring the vinegar and basil sprigs to a simmer. Remove from the heat and steep until cool. Strain and reserve. (This may be done well in advance and the sprigs stored in the refrigerator.)

2. Preheat oven to 350 F.

3. Spread the pine nuts in a single layer on a baking sheet and toast until golden brown (about 5 minutes). Check frequently to avoid burning.

4. Trim the watercress, discarding any wilted leaves and cutting off all but about 1 1/2 inches of the stems.

5. Cut the tomatoes into 1/4-inch-thick slices.

6. Cut the onions into 1/8-inch-thick slices and season with salt and cracked black pepper. Toss with 1/4 cup olive oil and grill over medium heat until lightly charred and wilted.

7. With a vegetable peeler, slice the cheese into ribbonlike curls and set aside.

To serve:

1. Chill six plates.

2. Toss the watercress with the vinaigrette and make a nest of it on each plate.

3. Arrange three large slices of tomato on top of the watercress in a circular pattern. Lightly sprinkle with salt, pepper, and sugar, then spoon a little of the basil-flavored red wine vinegar on top.

4. Place several rings of the grilled onions on top of the tomatoes and sprinkle with the toasted pine nuts. Arrange three ribbons of cheese on top of each salad. Drizzle with extra-virgin olive oil and garnish with a few basil leaves.

Steamed Lobster with Grapefruit Butter Sauce

Serves 4

4 lobsters, about 1 1/2 pounds each

Orzo

1 cup uncooked orzo	Pinch of freshly grated nutmeg
2 tablespoons Brown Butter (*see* recipe opposite)	Salt and white pepper to taste
2 tablespoons extra-virgin olive oil	

Spinach sauté

3 tablespoons butter	Pinch of freshly grated nutmeg
2 cups tightly packed spinach leaves, stems removed	Salt and freshly ground pepper to taste

Grapefruit Butter Sauce

Juice of 4 pink grapefruits	1 cup (2 sticks) cold unsalted butter, cut into tablespoon-size pieces
1 cup heavy cream	
3/4 cup chicken stock	Salt and white pepper to taste

Flavored liquid to rewarm the lobster

1 quart water	3 tablespoons butter
1 cup orange juice	

Grapefruit garnish

2 grapefruits, peeled and carefully sectioned, with pith removed

To cook the lobster:

1. Holding the lobsters with a kitchen towel, carefully pull off the claws.

2. In a large kettle or steamer, bring 2 inches of salted water to a rolling boil. Add the lobster bodies, cover, and cook for 1 minute. Add the claws, cover, and cook for 8 minutes more.

3. Remove the lobsters and claws from the steamer and plunge into ice water for 3 minutes to stop the cooking.

4. Remove the lobsters from the ice water. Pull out the tail and claw meat in whole pieces, using a mallet to crack the claws. Refrigerate the meat.

To cook the orzo:

1. In a large saucepan, bring 3 quarts of salted water to a rolling boil and add the orzo. Cook for 5 minutes, or until al dente.

2. Drain the orzo and transfer to a medium-sized bowl. Add the Brown Butter, oil, nutmeg, and salt and white pepper. Toss gently to coat the pasta evenly. Set aside and keep warm.

To make the spinach sauté:

In a large skillet, melt the butter over medium heat. When the butter begins to foam, add the spinach and quickly toss with tongs to coat evenly. Add the nutmeg and sea-

son with salt and pepper. Remove to a warm dish.

To make the Grapefruit Butter Sauce:

1. In a 2-quart heavy-bottomed saucepan, combine the grapefruit juice, cream, and stock. Cook over medium-high heat until the sauce has a syrupy consistency.

2. Whisk in the cold butter, 1 tablespoon at a time, until all the butter is incorporated. Season with salt and white pepper. Set aside and keep warm.

To serve:

1. In a 4-quart saucepan, combine 1 quart of water with the orange juice and butter. Bring to a simmer.

2. Drop the lobster meat into the pan and warm for 2 minutes.

3. Meanwhile, place a mound of the dressed orzo in the center of each of four hot serving plates.

4. Remove the lobster meat from the pan with a slotted spoon and distribute among the plates on top of the orzo. Garnish with grapefruit sections and spinach sauté and surround with Grapefruit Butter Sauce.

Note: The lobsters may be steamed and removed from their shells well in advance and kept refrigerated until ready to serve. The Grapefruit Butter Sauce may be made an hour or so ahead of time and kept warm in the top of a double boiler off the heat. Steamed white rice may be substituted for the orzo.

Brown Butter

Makes 1 cup

1/2 pound lightly salted butter

In a heavy skillet over medium heat, melt the butter, stirring constantly. Increase the heat and continue stirring as the butter foams and begins to turn golden brown. Immediately remove the butter from the heat and carefully pour it into a heat-proof container.

"Filet Mignon" of Rare Tuna Capped with Seared Foie Gras on Charred Onions and a Burgundy Butter Sauce

Serves 4

4 center-cut tuna steaks, about 6 ounces
    each, trimmed into the shape of
    filet mignon

1 large white onion, sliced 1/4-inch thick

1/4 cup olive oil (approximately)

2 large carrots, peeled and sliced very thin
    lengthwise into ribbons

2 medium zucchini, sliced very thin
    lengthwise into ribbons

2 tablespoons Brown Butter
    (*see* recipe on page 149)

Salt and freshly ground pepper to taste

4 ounces foie gras

Burgundy Butter Sauce (*see* recipe opposite)

1. Heat a 10-inch cast-iron skillet over high heat until very hot.

2. Moisten the onion slices with oil and lay in the hot skillet one layer deep. Cook until lightly charred, turn over with tongs, and char the other side. Remove from the pan and keep warm. Repeat until all the onion slices are cooked.

3. Meanwhile, bring about 2 quarts of lightly salted water to a rapid boil and drop in the carrot ribbons. Cook for 2 to 3 minutes, or until the carrots are tender but still al dente. Lift the carrots out of the water with a slotted spoon and place in a bowl. Using the same pot of boiling water, repeat this process with the zucchini ribbons. (*Note:* The zucchini will cook much faster than the carrots.)

4. Add the cooked zucchini to the carrots. Add the Brown Butter and season with salt and pepper.

5. Using a very sharp knife dipped in warm water, cut the foie gras into 1/2-inch-thick slices. Sprinkle with salt and pepper and keep chilled.

6. Moisten the tuna steaks with oil and season with salt and pepper. Place in the same hot skillet used to char the onions. Sear for about 2 minutes on each side. Remove and keep warm.

7. In a smoking-hot 7-inch sauté pan, sear the liver slices on both sides for about 30 seconds, or just until a crisp outer crust forms. Remove and keep warm.

To serve:

1. Quickly lay three or four charred onion rings in the center of each of four warm serving plates. Arrange two carrot ribbons and two zucchini ribbons over the onions in a nest-like pattern. Place a tuna steak on top, then finish with a slice of foie gras and a few charred onions.

2. Sauce each plate with three pools of Burgundy Butter Sauce.

Burgundy Butter Sauce

Makes 2 cups

1 cup balsamic vinegar

1 1/8 cups red wine

1 shallot, cut in half

1/4 cup (1/2 stick) cold unsalted butter, cut into tablespoon-size pieces

1/2 cup (1 stick) cold lightly salted butter, cut into tablespoon-size pieces

1. In a medium-sized heavy-bottomed saucepan, combine the vinegar, wine, and shallot over medium heat and reduce to a syrupy consistency.

2. Using a wooden spoon, incorporate the butter in the sauce one piece at a time. When all the butter is incorporated, remove the shallot pieces. Keep warm until ready to serve.

Silver Queen Corn Sauté

(A side dish)
Serves 6

6 ears fresh sweet corn
   (approximately 5 to 6 cups kernels)

4 strips bacon, diced

1 red bell pepper, finely diced

1 green bell pepper, finely diced

1 tablespoon balsamic vinegar

1 tablespoon sugar

Salt and freshly ground pepper to taste

1 1/2 tablespoons chopped fresh cilantro

1. Shuck the corn, brushing off all the silk. Strip the kernels off with a sharp knife.

2. In a 2-quart saucepan, blanch the bacon in boiling water for 1 minute. Drain and dry on a paper towel.

3. Place the bacon in a sauté pan and cook until crisp and brown. Using a slotted spoon, remove the bacon and pour off half the fat from the pan.

4. Add the red and green bell peppers to the pan and sweat over medium heat for about 2 minutes. Add the corn and sauté for 3 to 4 more minutes.

5. Add the balsamic vinegar, sugar, and salt and pepper. Return the bacon to the pan and add the cilantro.

6. Remove the corn mixture from the pan and keep warm until ready to serve.

Lemon-Rosemary Sorbet with Campari

Makes 2 1/2 quarts

2 quarts Simple Syrup (*see* recipe below)

1 cup fresh lemon juice

1/2 cup Campari

Pinch of salt

2 tablespoons finely chopped fresh rosemary

1 egg white, beaten until medium peaks form

1. In a medium-sized bowl, combine the Simple Syrup, lemon juice, Campari, salt, and rosemary.

2. Transfer to an ice cream machine. When the mixture becomes slushy, add the egg white. Freeze in the ice cream machine according to the manufacturer's instructions.

Simple Syrup

Makes 2 quarts

9 cups water   4 cups sugar

1. Combine the water and sugar in a heavy-bottomed saucepan over medium heat. Stir until the sugar is completely dissolved and the liquid is clear. Remove from the heat and cool to room temperature.

2. Store indefinitely in the refrigerator.

INDEX

"The dining experience can be a healing
process that makes you feel life is worth living."

—*Patrick O'Connell*